The
Fetishism
of Modernities

Frank M. Covey, Jr.
Loyola Lectures in Political Analysis

Thomas S. Engeman
General Editor

Our late colleague Richard S. Hartigan founded the Frank M. Covey, Jr., Lectures in Political Analysis to provide a continuing forum for the reanimation of political philosophy. The lectures are not narrowly constrained by a single topic nor do they favor a particular perspective. Their sole aim is to foster serious theoretical inquiry, with the expectation that this effort will contribute in essential ways to both human knowledge and political justice.

The Fetishism of Modernities

Epochal Self-Consciousness
in Contemporary Social
and Political Thought

Bernard Yack

UNIVERSITY OF NOTRE DAME PRESS
Notre Dame, Indiana

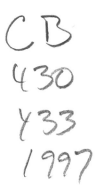

© 1997 by
University of Notre Dame Press
Notre Dame, Indiana 46556
All Rights Reserved.

Designed by Wendy McMillen
Set in 11/14 Adobe Caslon by The Book Page, Inc.
Printed in the U.S.A. by Thomson-Shore, Inc.

Library of Congress Cataloging-in-Publication Data

Yack, Bernard, 1952–
    The fetishism of modernities : epochal self-
consciousness in contemporary social and political
thought / Bernard Yack.
        p.   cm. — (Frank M. Covey, Jr. Loyola lectures in
political analysis)
    Includes bibliographical references and index.
    ISBN 0-268-02850-8 (cloth : alk. paper)
    1. Civilization, Modern—1950– —Philosophy.
2. Social sciences—Philosophy.   3. Postmodernism.
I. Title.   II. Series.
CB430.Y33   1997
301'.01—dc21   97-12144
                                                    CIP

For Marion

Contents

Acknowledgments

This book is a revised version of the Frank M. Covey Lectures that I presented at Loyola University of Chicago in March 1996. Although I have altered much of the original text, the five chapters of the book correspond to the topics of the five lectures I delivered at Loyola. I am very grateful to Thomas Engemann and Rob Mayer for the invitation to deliver these lectures and for the hospitality and stimulating conversation they and their colleagues provided during my visit. I would also like to thank many friends and scholars for their encouragement and helpful criticisms of my ideas about modernity: Mark Blitz, Richard Flathman, Don Herzog, Stephen Holmes, Claudio Katz, Richard Kraut, Jane Mansbridge, John Meyer, Jim Miller, Linda Nicholson, Robert Pippin, Richard Rorty, Steve Seidman, Gary Shiffman, and Robert Wokler. My greatest debt is, as always, to Marion Smiley, to whom I lovingly dedicate this book.

The Fetishism of Modernities and the Secret Thereof

> Raising these doubts is not a matter of denying the actual existence of various epochs; in a certain sense each is indeed based on a different kind of person; but it is a question of precisely this "certain sense."

Robert Musil, "Helpless Europe"

Contemporary intellectuals seem to be experiencing an acute outbreak of epochal self-consciousness. The agent of this contagion is an idea: that peculiarly expansive and evocative concept, modernity. Increasingly, we see important theoretical and practical issues debated in terms of whether modernity is dead, exhausted, incomplete, or merely misunderstood, rather than in terms of the value of the particular insights or practices in question. Modernity, it seems, has become the leading character in the drama of our time. Indeed, I would suggest that it is only an obsession with a particular way of thinking about modernity that has turned our relatively stable and neatly ordered corner of Western history into a drama in the minds of so many contemporary intellectuals.

After all, there is little in our everyday lives—apart from the coming millennium—to inspire speculation about the passing of epochs, at least in the prosperous Western nations in which such speculation is now rampant. The dramatic events and wrenching transformations that have inspired epochal speculation in the past, the collapse of empires and civilizations, revolutionary upheavals, devastating wars or natural disasters, the rise of new religions and charismatic leaders, do not loom large on our horizon. Even the recent collapse of Soviet communism, which most resembles such events, is generally experienced as the end of an interruption of normal historical developments, as a "return to history," rather than as a break with the past.

Nor is there much evidence that dissatisfaction with characteristically modern ideas and institutions is reaching an epoch-making level of depth and intensity. Antimodern sentiments were far more powerful and intense earlier in this century than they are now. In the aftermath of the mindless slaughter of World War I, for example, faith in progress was reduced to a laughable vice; Fascist parties mobilized resentment against the modern world into successful mass movements; and many of Europe's most influential intellectuals declared themselves ready to "side with the men who made Socrates drink hemlock."[1] Today, in contrast, antimodern sentiments have relatively little impact on mass politics in the liberal democracies, and very few intellectuals seem willing to join forces with their executioners, no matter how much these intellectuals may condemn the Enlightenment.

What then has changed to set off the current outbreak of epochal speculation? First of all, there is the widespread shift from modernist to postmodernist styles in the arts. It is not at all unreasonable to believe that the waning of aesthetic modernism marks the end of an epoch in the history of some forms of art and literature, especially architecture and music. And from the end of an epoch in artistic expression it is a short leap to thoughts about the end of an epoch in human history, especially when we are accustomed to using artistic styles to classify past epochs, as in talk of the "Baroque" or "Classical" eras.

Second, and perhaps more important, there is the rise to prominence of a new critique of modern ideas and institutions, a critique that its advocates tend to identify with the shift from modernist to postmodernist aesthetics. Earlier critics of modernity tended, if anything, to exaggerate the power of distinctively modern ideas and institutions. They asked themselves how to resist or radicalize the forces of change modernity had introduced into our lives. Postmodern critics, in contrast, tend to treat modernity as a spent force, a process of change that is collapsing in exhaustion or self-contradiction. They ask themselves instead how are we going to live in a world in which characteristically modern ideas and institutions are increasingly ineffective and unsatisfying.

It is this claim about "the end of modernity" that has made contemporary intellectuals so acutely self-conscious about their place in history.[2] On the one hand, it has set off a mad scramble of speculation about what forms of life lie in wait for us across "the postmodern divide,"[3] speculation about the coming postmodern forms of everything from physics and commerce to the family and the American presidency. On the other hand, this claim has inspired numerous attempts to reconstruct modernity in a way that would sustain its progressive dynamism without promoting the kind of self-destructive practices that postmodernists rightly condemn. Habermas's vision of modernity as an "unfinished project" is just the best known of these alternative conceptions of modernity.[4] In the midst of so much speculation about the true shape of the modern and postmodern worlds, epochal self-consciousness is all but unavoidable for the contemporary intellectual.

It is odd, however, that the current obsession with modernity should be inspired by the ideas of the very people who, one would think, should be the most suspicious of it: the postmodernists. For few ideas would seem to present a more inviting target for postmodern criticism than the concept of modernity. Distilling whole centuries of human experience into a single, coherent vision of life would seem to violate almost every canon of postmodernist reasoning. Such a vision represents ideas and institutions as a totality rather than as a diverse assortment of social practices and language games. It assumes that individuals can gain an external perspective on their practices and thereby identify them as part of a single, decaying epoch. And, worst of all, it integrates our experience into precisely the kind of grand historical narratives that postmodernists ordinarily condemn.

Nevertheless, few ideas play a more prominent role in postmodernist discourse than the concept of modernity. "Modernity ends," writes one influential postmodernist philosopher, "when it is no longer possible to treat history as unilinear."[5] But what meaning can the statement "modernity ends" have outside of a view of history in which human experience unfolds in a single direction? And how can one talk about the "end of modernity" without treating modern experience as a highly integrated and coherent whole? At the very least, "discussions of post-modernity presuppose that our age is unified enough to speak of its ending."[6]

In spite of their vaunted skepticism, there is one grand narrative that many postmodernists seem to cling to: a story about the rise and fall of the collective condition known as modernity. But they cannot do so without relying upon precisely the kind of claim that their critique of foundationalism and grand historical narratives rules out: that it makes sense to treat a whole epoch of human experience as a single stage in the unfolding development of human culture.[7] Accepting this critique should spell the end of our *illusions* about the coherence and integrity of modern experience, rather than the end of modernity itself. For if postmodernists are right about social plurality and fragmentation, then modernity should be viewed as a "never was" rather than a "has been."[8]

But far from treating modernity as a "never was," many postmodernists join Jean-François Lyotard in constructing a grand counternarrative about modernity. In this counternarrative, the assertion of rationalism becomes a self-destructive project of human emancipation, a project that leads from the intellectual innovations of Plato or Descartes through the emergence of technology and rationalized bureaucracy to the death camps of Auschwitz and the Gulag. Twentieth-century genocide and totalitarianism are portrayed in this story as the completion of the processes set in motion by the project of modern rationalism. In the ruins of the modern project, we are told, we have no sane choice but to "wage war on [the] terror" associated with rationalism and universalism in order to "liberate the differences" and "defend the honor of the name" that they seek to suppress.[9]

This is quite a powerful story. It is not at all surprising that it attracts so many followers. But it is just that: a story, and quite a grand story at that, not at all the kind of local knowledge and *petits recits* celebrated by Lyotard and his followers. It is a tale about the hidden truth of modernity, a metanarrative about the self-destructive core at the heart of modern efforts to emancipate individuals from authority and suffering. Loath to abandon a role in this drama, many postmodernists seem willing to overlook their usual suspicion of grand historical narratives and social totalities when they talk about the rise and fall of modernity. They may have abandoned Marx's theories about "the fetishism of commodities and the secret thereof,"[10] but they persist in what I call the *fetishism of modernities*, a way of thinking that, I shall try to show, was promoted by Marx and other nineteenth-century philosophers and social theorists.

The fetishism of modernities is a "social myth" that "unifies many-sided social processes and phenomena into a single grand object."[11] Once we construct such an object, it tends to take on a life of its own as the leading character in our historical dramas. And before long we are speculating about subjects like modernity's needs, modernity's projects, and even its tragic failings. For these grand objects promise to unlock the secrets of the "history behind history,"[12] to unearth the deeper forces that explain the booming, buzzing confusion of everyday life.

Postmodernists are famous for their scathing critiques of such "grand objects" and the historical metanarratives that grow up around them. But in insisting that we are leaving modernity behind and entering a new "postmodern condition" many postmodernists, like Lyotard, retain these objects and merely change the stories they tell about them. The secret of our current obsession with the fate of modernity is the persistent tendency of many contemporary intellectuals, including some of the most adamant opponents of the idea of totality, to treat the human condition in recent centuries as a coherent and integrated whole.

Here is a particularly striking example of the fetishism of modernities. It is taken from Herbert Marcuse's *One-Dimensional Man:*

> Advanced industrial society . . . is the realization of a specific historical project. . . . As that project unfolds it shapes the entire universe of discourse and action, interests and material culture. In the medium of technology, culture, politics, and

the economy merge into an omnipresent system which swallows up or repulses all alternatives.[13]

Marcuse's words provide a good indication of the way in which the fetishism of modernities influences a thinker. One begins with a sense of what is most *distinctive* about modern existence, in this case the set of practices identified as "advanced industrial society." But one ends up insisting that this distinctive set of ideas and institutions informs "the *entire* universe of discourse and action, interests and material culture" in the modern period.

I call this treatment of modern experience as a coherent and integrated whole a "fetishism" in order to highlight the way in which, like Marx's fetishism of commodities, it encourages us to treat our own creations as if they have a life of their own. Modernity, the modern condition, the spirit of modern life, these are intellectual inventions inspired by our need to come to grips with the unprecedented social and cultural transformations of recent centuries. We come up with these ideas by focussing our attention on the most distinctive features of recent social experience and by consciously abstracting from the great range of ideas and institutions that do not share these features. But by treating modernity as a coherent and integrated whole we turn these *distinguishing* features of modern life and thought into a condition that shapes *all* aspects of modern experience. In this way, our own intellectual inventions come back to haunt us as an omnipresent force in our lives.[14]

Treating the modern age as a coherent and integrated whole does not require that one view it as a harmonious unity. Indeed, the idea of modernity as an integrated and coherent condition was first developed by philosophers and social critics who sought to identify the fundamental divisions—subject/object, private/public, inclination/duty,

bourgeois/proletariat, and so on—that they believed struc-
tured modern life and thought.[15] If one argues that a single
set of contradictions explains the character and prospects
of modern life, then one is still treating modernity as a coherent and integrated whole, no matter how much one may
complain about the lack of personal and social harmony in
the modern world. Alternatively, by pointing to deeper,
more fundamental characteristics that are shared by the
most irreconcilable enemies in the modern world, one can
treat modernity as a coherent and integrated whole without
denying the conflict and competition within our experience. Currently, the most influential example of this version of the fetishism of modernities is Heidegger's erasure
of the opposition between Nazism, Soviet communism, and
liberal democracy. All of these implacable enemies, Heidegger insists, "stand under the same reality": the insatiable
will to power expressed by the technological drive to dominate the earth.[16] Whatever division and disharmony we
experience thus merely hides the deeper, more fundamental
coherence and integrity of the modern world.

I speak of a fetishism of modernit*ies* because there are as
many "modernities" as there are understandings about what
is most distinctive about modern life and experience. The
fetishism of modernities develops when we read one of
these understandings—such as the disenchantment of the
world, the attempt to conquer nature, the rise of industrial
society, or the experience of transitoriness—into the structure of modern life and experience as a whole.

Finally, I speak of the fetishism of modernities as a "tendency," rather than as an opinion or a theory, because
few contemporary theorists are willing to explicitly endorse the description of modernity as a coherent and integrated whole, especially now with the concept of "totality"
in such disrepute.[17] Nevertheless, this way of thinking about

modernity still plays a powerful, if unacknowledged, role in most contemporary debates about modernity. Without it many of the most familiar moves in these debates would lose their powerful impact on the minds of contemporary intellectuals.

Take, for example, Martin Heidegger's famous critique of modern technology. Heidegger describes modernity as "the age of consummate meaninglessness," an age in which "worldviews are invented and promulgated with a view to their power" to transform the world and serve human needs.[18] The conquest of nature looms large in this portrait of the modern age. But Heidegger insists that technology and all of its enormous impact on the world are the fruit of a much more fundamental change, a shift in the way in which being has been addressed and received by great thinkers. Accordingly, he argues that it is metaphysics that "grounds" the modern age and "gives to that age the basis . . . [that] holds complete dominion over *all* the phenomena that distinguish the age" (emphasis added).[19]

Heidegger argues that the "specific comprehension of truth" that dominates our age leads us to treat all of existence as a mere "standing-reserve," a collection of discrete things ready to be measured by our needs and calculations.[20] Our great technological projects are merely the most spectacular consequence of this new way of thinking, although one that Heidegger dwells upon at length:

> What the river is now, namely a water power supplier, derives from out of the essence of the power station. In order that we may even remotely consider the monstrousness that reigns here, let us ponder for a moment the contrast that speaks out of the two titles, "The Rhine" as dammed up into the *power* works, and "The Rhine" as uttered out of the *art* work, in Hölderlin's hymn by that name. But, it will be replied,

the Rhine is still a river in the landscape, is it not? Perhaps. But how? In *no other way* than as an object on call for inspection by a tour group ordered there by the vacation industry.[21]

Most readers, including, I suspect, even the majority of Heideggerians, would recognize an element of exaggeration in these statements and mentally discount them, even if they found them inspiring. Surely, at least at times, we look at the Rhine, at mountains, at the ocean, at the countless stars in the sky as something more than material ready at hand to serve our interests in power, calculation, or edification. But the deep impact of statements such as these depends precisely on the way in which they tend to fill the whole horizon of modern life and experience. "Monstrousness" reigns in the image of the Rhine river hydroelectric works only to the extent that we believe that in the modern world we can view nature "in *no other way* than as an object on call" to our needs. It is not the simple act of subordinating nature to human purpose and calculation that is monstrous (unless, unlike Heidegger, one believes that nature has a right to be treated as an end in itself). It is rather the crowding out of all other ways of relating to being that is so frightening in the vision that Heidegger evokes.[22]

The impact of such visions depends upon an unstated background assumption that the modern age forms a coherent and integrated whole, an assumption that few contemporary intellectuals, unlike Marcuse and many of his generation, would endorse were they asked to do so. In this way, as a tendency or an implicit assumption, the fetishism of modernities has survived, even thrived, in contemporary debates about modernity. Ironically, intellectuals have never been more obsessed with this way of thinking about modernity than they are now when they are more hostile than ever to the concept of social totality that sustains it.

I believe that it is therefore high time to subject the concept of modernity to a sustained critical examination. There has been relatively little discussion of the viability of the concept of modernity itself,[23] despite the ongoing debate about the origins, content, and viability of modernity as a way of life and thought. The participants in these debates seem to take the existence of their object, modernity, for granted. They rarely try to figure out in precisely what ways it makes sense to speak of the disparate phenomena they discuss as part of a single epoch. These days few would disagree, least of all postmodernists, that "we need to discourage the desire to find one deep pattern [in modern experience] that lets us understand everything else."[24] But until we take some time out to examine the concept of modernity itself, as opposed to competing conceptions of modernity, I am afraid that this desire will continue to burn and smolder, no matter how many times we attempt to douse it with violent denunciations of totality.

It is not my goal, however, to eliminate the concept of modernity from contemporary discourse. (As if I could!) I undertake this critique of the idea of modernity in order to promote a clearer and more realistic understanding of the nature and influence of distinctly modern ideas and practices in our lives, not merely to provide additional illustrations of the penchant of modern intellectuals for deluding themselves. Like Hans Blumenberg, I am looking to establish the conditions for "a more realistic use of the concept of a [modern] epoch."[25] I am very sympathetic to postmodernists' rejection of grand historical narratives and celebrations of totality. But I believe that "in a certain sense" it is still plausible and enlightening to characterize recent centuries in terms of distinctively modern ideas and practices.[26] The challenge is to identify this "certain sense" and distinguish it from conceptualizations of modernity as a coherent and integrated whole.

This is not to say that I am trying to identify the *real* epochal breaks in historical experience *wie es eigentlich gewesen war.* All periodizations of history are, needless to say, intellectual constructions. Unmasking them as such only brings us back to questions about how consistent, plausible, and enlightening each particular construction may be. I am worried that in current debates about modernity we often mistake an intellectual construction for a worldly reality. But my deeper concern is that this particular construction that we have been relying upon is getting increasingly inconsistent, implausible, and unenlightening.

Treating an epoch as a coherent and integrated whole can have enormous heuristic value. It can draw our attention to unsuspected connections between seemingly discrete attitudes and spheres of activity; it can establish the basis for enlightening comparative analysis of ideas and institutions; and it can serve as a continual reminder of the importance of historical context to thought and action. But I fear that with the fetishism of modernities this particular treatment of modern phenomena is no longer paying its way. Like the idea of a crisis of our time, this way of thinking about modernity has become "a stale platitude, obscuring more layers of reality, more aspects of experience, than it reveals." Designed originally to make sense of new and surprising developments, it ends up providing us instead with "the comfort of recognition,"[27] as we ease our surprise and bewilderment by assimilating these developments into familiar models of modern—and, increasingly, postmodern—thought and behavior.

In this study I try to show that treating modernity as a coherent and integrated whole blinds us to some of the most interesting and important aspects of the world around us: for example, the surprising role of reverence for tradition in modern political life, a crucial component, I argue, of liberal constitutionalism, among other things; the development of new ideas and practices that are *not* reducible to modern—or, for that matter, postmodern—models of thought and behavior, which is how I shall interpret nationalism, among other things; and perhaps most surprising, the very uniqueness of the distinctively modern ideas and practices that inspired the idea of modernity in the first place. In the end, the fetishism of modernities filters out much of what is most unexpected, incongruous, and just plain interesting in our experience.

In the first chapter, "Imagining the Modern Age," I explore the use and abuse of modernity as a synonym for the modern age or modern condition. In the second chapter, "From the Moderns to Modernity," I discuss the two most important and influential sources of the idea of modernity as a coherent and integrated whole: post-Kantian German philosophy and classical nineteenth-century social theory.

Chapter 3 focuses on the shortcomings of the idea that we are entering a new, postmodern social condition. Let me make clear now that my argument in this chapter is addressed against the idea of *postmodernity,* rather than against the set of loosely connected theories and styles collected under the heading of *postmodernism.* As I have already noted, I have considerable sympathy for postmodernist objections to foundationalism and totalizing philosophies of history. But the idea of postmodernity or an emergent "postmodern condition," I argue in Chapter 3, only makes sense in terms of precisely the kind of totalistic thinking about social relations that postmodernists regularly denounce. To be more precise, it makes sense only on the assumption that modernity forms a coherent and integrated whole, which is why I describe postmodernity in the title of that chapter as "a figment of a fetish."

Postmodernists might respond to this argument by denying that it makes any sense to single out any particular stories about the modern world as myths or fetishes, since we only have access to the world through the stories we tell about it, and we can only measure the value of these stories by their ability to empower and edify, rather than by the accuracy of their claims. If Lyotard and others end up constructing a grand philosophic narrative about modernity, so much the better, they might argue, as long as it empowers the right kind of people and causes. Such arguments represent the side of postmodernism for which I have decidedly less sympathy—and not only because of the annoying way in which they absolve postmodernists of the most basic requirements of moral and intellectual consistency.

Postmodernism, it seems to me, is driven by two competing insights: one forces us to pay closer attention to the richness and complexity of worldly experience; the other frees us from this obligation. The first of these insights maintains that the world is too complex and inconsistent to be captured by the grand narratives of progress and human emancipation that have sustained so many modern ideas and institutions. The second maintains that because of this complexity our accounts of the world must be measured by their ability to empower and edify, rather than enlighten and explain. The first insight compels us to pay closer attention to the world in order to capture the complexities and inconsistencies that are obscured by foundationalism and grand philosophies of history. The second insight, however, allows us to turn away from the richness of actual human experience and construct narratives that distort reality as much as the foundationalist narratives about modernity that postmodernists spend so much time criticizing. Indeed, as I have suggested, it may even allow one to revive totalizing grand narratives about modernity, as long as one takes an ironic attitude toward them.[28]

This second insight about story-telling edification makes the idea of "distorting reality" seem incoherent. Nevertheless, I believe that it is precisely the distortion of reality and the misrepresentation of actual human experience that inspires the postmodern critique of foundationalism and grand philosophies of history in the first place. Postmodernists may not be in a position to provide a consistent account of the basic structure of real-world actions and experience. But they should stand firm in insisting on the way in which grand narratives about modernity and humanity distort and misrepresent the world. That is why I believe that postmodernists, above all others, should recognize that the idea of postmodernity is nothing but a figment of a fetish that they have sought to expose and eliminate.

In Chapter 4, to return to my summary, I address the question of what is modern and what is not in liberal democracy. Liberal democracy is often portrayed as the distinctively modern political regime. But once we abandon the tendency to treat modernity as an integrated and coherent whole, it begins to look much more inconsistent and, I try to show, much more interesting. Finally, in Chapter 5 I try to show that the fetishism of modernities has promoted wildly exaggerated ideas about the power of modern theory to shape, and misshape modern practice. My primary targets in this chapter are Heidegger's critique of modern science and technology and Adorno's and Horkheimer's famous critique of the Enlightenment. My aim is to disentangle modern theory and practice in order to help us better explain and deal with some of the distinctive features of modern life and thought.

As this outline should indicate, this essay takes the form of a series of arguments, rather than a series of commentaries on different thinkers. Many of the big names, such as Hegel and Marx, Habermas and Heidegger, will come up for consideration, but only as illustrations of my arguments rather than as the subject of detailed commentary. I have learned a great deal from the thoughts of Hegel and his successors about the nature of the modern world. But I have noted already, while a great deal of excellent work has been done on their differing *conceptions* of modernity,[29] little has been done to think through the concept of modernity itself. The latter is the task that I have set for myself in this study.

One

Imagining the Modern Age

The modern age was the first and only age that understood itself as an epoch and, in so doing, simultaneously created the other epochs.

Hans Blumenberg, *The Legitimacy of the Modern Age*

Speaking of Modernity

Like all classificatory concepts, epoch categories tempt us to exaggerate the uniformity that exists within specific areas of our social experience. We construct these concepts in order to focus attention on differences and divisions, such as the tension between different ways of life, the succession of different modes of organization, and the contrast between competing styles of artistic expression. But highlighting such distinctions in this way often leads us to exaggerate the coherence and integrity of the social experiences contained within the boundaries that we have constructed.

This kind of exaggeration is to some extent unavoidable. It is part of the price we pay for the conceptual maps without which we could never navigate through everyday life, let alone begin to offer explanations of the way things are. An omniscient being could know everything in its distinctness and particularity. We mere mortals cannot, for we cannot look in every direction at once. Our classificatory concepts tend to exaggerate differences and similarities; but we need these exaggerations in order to learn about the distinct qualities of things.

What I am calling the fetishism of modernities might seem, at first glance, to be little more than a particularly powerful and influential example of this kind of exaggeration. As such, it might seem to call merely for reminders of the provisional and heuristic nature of the epoch categories and ideal types we associate with the term modernity. No doubt, much of the current tendency to treat modernity as a coherent and integrated whole can be addressed in this way. But I believe that there is something more to the fetishism of modernities than this familiar problem with the use of classificatory concepts, something specific to the way in which we speak about modernity.

Consider, for example, the following description of modernity from the opening pages of William Connolly's book *Political Theory and Modernity:*

> Or perhaps modernity is the *epoch in which* the destruction of the world followed the collective attempt to master it. . . . Even if modernity is not unique (it is too early to tell), it is at least distinctive. In its optimistic moments it *defines itself* by contrast to earlier periods which are darker, more superstitious, less free, less rational, less productive, less civilized, less comfortable, less democratic, less tolerant, less respectful of the individual, less scientific and less developed technically than it is at its best. *Its opponents* often endorse these differentiations while grading them differently. . . . If *modernity strives to perfect* agencies of change and progress, the locus, ends and means of agency become objects of debate.[1] (Emphasis added)

Connolly begins by talking about modernity as a period of time, "the epoch in which" a momentous event, the destruction of the natural world we moderns have sought to master, may soon take place. As such, modernity is a very inclusive concept. Defenders and critics of modern science, for example, belong equally to modernity understood in this way, since they both emerge within the period of time that we describe as modern. But Connolly quickly shifts to a different way of talking about modernity: as a particular way of being and thinking, one that "defines itself" and its times as an effort to master nature, "strives to perfect agencies of change and progress," and has numerous "opponents" who reject its goals and values. Understood in this way, modernity is a much narrower concept. Only those ideas and institutions that are in some important sense informed by a distinctly modern set of goals and values belong to modernity. In the first instance, the boundaries of modernity are temporal and rather broad; everything within the current epoch is appropriately characterized as modern. In the second instance, its boundaries are substantive and relatively exclusive; modernity is an ideal type that allows us to identify and distinguish certain qualities of life and thought that have become prominent within the modern epoch.

Unfortunately, the English language offers nothing like the contrast in German between *die Neuzeit* (the new or modern age) and *die Modernität* (modernity or the quality of being modern) to keep these two ways of speaking about modernity distinct. In English these days we tend to use the term modernity to characterize distinctive ways of being in the world as well as a particular period of time. Modernity for us denotes both the peculiar qualities of life in a world of alarm clocks, subways, and eighty-story office buildings and the epoch in which such a life becomes prominent. We use the term both as a synonym for expressions such as the modern age or modern times and to signify the distinctive quality of certain ideas, styles, and practices that have emerged during this period of time.

Both of these uses of the term modernity are relatively new developments, although the use of modernity to designate the modern epoch is the more recent. While the term modern has a long and continuous history of usage going back at least to the fifth century, the term modernity has become popular, despite some appearances in eleventh-century Latin texts, only in the last 150 years.[2] It is usually described as a French coinage of Chateaubriand, popularized by Baudelaire as part of his effort to put his finger on the special quality of modern life captured by new forms of art and literature.[3] (It should be noted, however, that the *OED* identifies English uses of the term modernity back as far as 1647, where it refers to a distinctive quality rather than to an epoch.) Only in the twentieth century has modernity become a widely used synonym for modern times or the modern age.[4]

Contemporary debates about modernity derive much of their significance from this ambiguity in the meaning of the term. What, for example, is the subject of Jürgen Habermas's influential book *The Philosophical Discourse of Modernity*? Is the book about the most important forms of philosophy that have emerged in recent years, i.e., the philosophic discourse *of* the modern age? Or is its subject recent theories of modernity, i.e., philosophic discourse *about* modernity? And if its subject is philosophic discourse about modernity, what is the focus of that discourse: the examination and evaluation of the epoch or of some distinctive qualities of thought and action that emerge within it? Frankly, I believe that Habermas's book deals with all of these subjects. One might have thought he could have avoided this ambiguity by making use of the German distinction between *Neuzeit* and *Modernität*. But Habermas uses a third term, *die Moderne*, in the title of his book, a term that is also translated most often as modernity.[5] This term reproduces the ambiguity of the English term modernity, which suggests that our difficulties with the term represent something more than a unfortunate dearth of words in the English language.

This ambiguity is especially striking in familiar expressions such as "the project" or "the crisis of modernity." Is the "project of modernity" the most striking and influential collective enterprise of the modern age or is it a shared effort to promote a particular way of acting and thinking called modernity? Does the "crisis of modernity" point to the end of the modern epoch or the breakdown of this particular way of thinking and acting? These expressions suggest both of these meanings to us—and not only because we use the term modernity in both a temporal and substantive sense, but also because of the widespread belief that it is the emergence and triumph of the distinctly modern quality of thought and action that gives the modern age its distinctive character.

A term like antiquity also refers to both a quality of things and to an epoch. But no one would confuse the two, since no one sees the quality of antiquity as the distinguishing feature of the ancient epoch. "Ancientness," the quality of being old, of being passed on to us from earlier times, is certainly something that *we* attribute to the things that we inherit from the epoch called classical antiquity. But there is not now, nor was there ever, a strong sense that this sense of being old defined the characteristic features of ancient life and thought in the way that the sense of modernity is said to define them in the modern age.[6] The crisis of antiquity, if it makes sense to talk about such a thing, was a problem with military preparedness or moral education or religious sensibilities, not a crisis in a distinctly ancient quality of life. The crisis *of* modernity, the difficulties that threaten to end our age in the way that the collapse of the western Roman Empire ended classical antiquity, is often portrayed, in contrast, as a crisis *in* modernity, a collapse of faith in the sense of being modern.

What are the costs of conflating these two different concepts of modernity, beyond a certain lack of clarity in our social analyses? The temporal and the substantive concepts of modernity each have important uses on their own. But conflating them makes us comfortable with a vision of modernity as a coherent and integrated whole, even if we would never explicitly endorse such a way of talking about modern ideas and institutions. For when we slip casually back and forth between these two ways of talking about modernity, we begin to associate a distinctively modern way of being and thinking with the modern epoch as a whole, as if distinctly modern qualities filled the whole horizon of experience within the period of time we call modernity.

Consider, in this light, Connolly's suggestion that "in modernity modernization is always under way."[7] If Connolly were invoking only the *substantive* concept of modernity as a distinctive condition or quality of life, this claim would be plausible but tautological, for it would tell us merely that wherever we find distinctively modern forms of existence we will also find processes of modernization. If he were invoking only the *temporal* concept of modernity as the current epoch, then this claim would be highly significant but wildly implausible, since it would suggest that *everywhere* we look in the modern age we will find processes of modernization. But because he shifts back and forth between these two ways of talking about modernity and blurs the distinction between them, this claim seems both significant and plausible. It gains its plausibility from the invocation of the substantive concept of modernity, its significance from the invocation of the temporal or epochal concept.

Clearly, modernization is *not always* under way in the modern age. There are many aspects of our lives that resist or are indifferent to the processes of change unleashed by distinctly modern ideas and practices. But when we blur the distinction between the temporal and substantive concepts of modernity, it is easy to lose sight of this obvious fact and to begin talking about modernity as if it formed a coherent and integrated whole governed by processes of modernization, even when we vehemently reject the idea of a social totality. Likewise, conflating these two concepts of modernity tends to blind us to all of the important and fascinating tensions between distinctly modern and non-modern ways of doing things that, as we shall see, sustain much of our cultural and political life.

If I am right about this problem, then there may appear to be a relatively simple remedy for the fetishism of modernities: rigorously separate these two ways of talking about modernity. Perhaps we would be better off if we stuck to older expressions like "the modern age" or "modern times" when talking about the current epoch. For if we insist that "modernity is a quality, not an epoch,"[8] we might be less prone to treating it as a coherent and integrated whole. Moreover, with this distinction firmly in mind, we could pursue distinctly modern (and, for that matter, postmodern) qualities of mind and action in whatever epoch they may arise, since we would no longer identify them exclusively with a particular period of time.[9]

Unfortunately, the remedy for the fetishism of modernities is not so simple. Our difficulty with the concept of modernity is a problem with a way of thinking, not just a contingent way of speaking. The fetishism of modernities arose long before modernity emerged as a synonym for the modern age, as I shall try to show in the following chapter.

We are not inclined to conflate the temporal and substantive concepts of modernity simply because we happen by chance to employ the same word to characterize them both. We employ the same term for these two ways of conceptualizing modernity because of the plausible connections between them. The temporal concept of modernity suggests the substantive because of the widespread belief that the modern epoch was initiated by distinctly modern ideas and practices, the belief that the emergence of these ideas and practices is a striking and significant enough turn of events to mark the beginning of a new, modern epoch. And the substantive concept of modernity suggests the temporal because "the consciousness of modernity" usually involves "the feeling of having broken with the past."[10] Modernity, as a distinctive quality of life and thought, makes us aware of our place in the flow of time in a way that the characteristic qualities that we attribute other epochs, such as classical antiquity, do not. As a result, the reach for epochal significance seems to be built into the substantive concept of modernity.

Even if we could stop using modernity as a synonym for the modern age, these plausible connections between the two concepts of modernity would still tempt us to treat the modern age as a coherent and integrated whole. Distinguishing the temporal and substantive concepts of modernity is an important first step toward moving beyond the fetishism of modernities. But we will not escape its influence until we begin to think through the way in which we imagine the modern age and its connection to the distinctive qualities we associate with the term modernity. Nevertheless, for clarity's sake, I shall try to use the term primarily in the substantive sense and to employ terms like the modern age or modern epoch to express the temporal concept of modernity. In this way it becomes much easier to discuss the relationship between distinctly modern qualities and the modern age, much easier than it would be if we had to deal with these issues as the relationship between two different concepts of modernity.

Temporal and Substantive Conceptions of the Modern Age

As we have seen, although the term modern is most commonly associated with time, it is invoked to answer "What?" as well as "When?" questions. We ascribe modernity to ideas, practices, and events with reference to some distinct quality that they possess as well as with reference to their temporal location. We do the same, I suggest, when imagining modernity as an epoch. Sometimes we emphasize our place in the flow of time when talking about the modern age, sometimes we emphasize distinctive modes of thought and action as a way of dividing time into periods. So let us begin by distinguishing between temporal and substantive conceptions of the modern age. The idea of modernity as an integrated and coherent whole conflates these two conceptions, each of which is quite plausible on its own.

The temporal conception of the modern age is the simplest and the most familiar. We tend to invoke this conception when we talk about "our times" or "the modern world." It represents the modern age as the period of time on the current side of some perceived disruption of historical continuity. Where we locate this discontinuity—1492, 1648, 1789, 1914, 1945, 1989—will change as time passes. But the modern epoch, according to this conception, has a clear and definite boundary: the date of the events that disrupted our sense of continuity with the past. *Everything* that happens after that date, whether it accelerates or reverses the forces of change, is equally part of the modern age. Living in the modern age, according to this conception, simply means existing on the current side of our most recent important break with the past.

The substantive conception of the modern age is somewhat less commonplace but plays a larger role in scholarly and intellectual discourse. We tend to invoke this conception of the modern age when we talk about the "modern condition" or "the experience of modernity," or any other time we are focusing our attention on what it means to live with the consequences of distinctly modern ideas and practices. It represents the modern age as the period of time in which distinctively modern ideas and practices rise to prominence. The modern age, according to this conception, lacks the clear and definite boundaries it has according to the temporal conception, since it is measured from the time these ideas and practices come to be significant forces in our lives, rather than from the specific date of their invention. Moreover, *everything* that happens within this period of time is not equally modern, since many of our attitudes and experiences will lack the characteristic qualities of these distinctly modern ideas and practices, even though they develop at the same time as others that possess these qualities. Living in the modern age, according to this conception, means living *with* the consequences of distinctively modern ideas and practices, rather than merely existing on the current side of some disruption of historical continuity.

Many ideas and institutions that are modern according to the temporal conception of the modern age are not modern according to the substantive conception. When, for example, we describe new fundamentalist sects as modern forms of religion, we are invoking the temporal conception of the modern age, since many of these sects are violently opposed to the kind of rational self-assertion that distinguishes most substantive conceptions of modernity. These sects are modern only in the sense that they emerge after the discontinuity that is treated as the beginning of the modern age.[11] Nor are all substantively modern phenomena also temporally modern. It all depends on where we draw the line between the current period and the past. If we draw that line, say, after the French Revolution, many of the most distinctively modern moves in philosophy, science, and social criticism will occur before the modern age begins. In that case, distinctly modern ideas and institutions can come to be perceived as relics of a past age, as many postmodernists now insist that they should be perceived.

Each of these two conceptions of the modern age is plausible and defensible on its own. The temporal conception represents the modern age as the new time *(Neuzeit)*, as the sum of all that develops on the current side of a dividing line that we draw in our recollection of past events. This conception of the modern age grows out of the kind of experience that leads one to say that "things will never be the same again," as people have often said to themselves after terrible events, such as World War I or the Holocaust, or after startling new discoveries, such as the existence of the American continents. Retrospectively, this conception grows out of our designation of some past event or discovery as the watershed after which things have never been the same. A precondition for thinking about the present time in this way is the rejection of the cyclical thinking about history favored by the ancient Greeks, among other cultures.[12] For as long as one thinks of history in cyclical terms, the experience of discontinuity is more likely to inspire the thought that "what goes around comes around" than the belief that nothing will ever be the same again.

The substantive conception of the modern age, like talk of the Age of Enlightenment or the Romantic era, employs a characteristic attitude, style, or activity to divide history into distinct periods. In this conception the modern age no more refers to the sum of all that develops within these centuries than the Age of Enlightenment refers to the sum of all the new developments in eighteenth-century Europe. It refers, instead, to a period of time distinguished by the prominence and influence of distinctly modern ideas and practices.[13] This conception grows out of our impression of the unprecedented power and influence of certain new ideas and practices, rather than from the shattering experience of some disruption of historical continuity.

Of course, thinking about the modern age in one way can start one off thinking about it in the other. If one experiences a sharp break in historical continuity, one is likely to begin to wonder about the distinctive qualities of life on the current side of that divide. And if one has a strong sense of the distinctiveness of modern life, then one is likely to look for the break with the past that initiated that new way of life, especially when so many key figures in modern thought understand themselves as initiating such a break.

But the two ways of conceptualizing the modern age do not logically entail each other. According to the temporal conception we live in the wake of a historical break after which things will never be the same again. But that does not mean that things have to *share* any consistent or even complementary qualities. Things may never be the same again in hundreds of different and conflicting ways. Conversely, the rise of distinctively modern ways of life need not grow out of a sense of a decisive break with the past. Locating the decisive moment of the "birth of modernity" may help us dramatize our stories about the rise of modern ideas and practices, but it always exaggerates the importance of particular dates and events in the evolution of the distinctive conditions we associate with modernity.[14]

Neither the temporal nor the substantive conceptions portray the modern age as an integrated and coherent whole. The temporal conception characterizes *all* new phenomena as modern, but without making any assertions about their coherence or integrity. The substantive conception locates in recent times a coherent core of modern ideas and practices, but only by denying that all the new phenomena surrounding that core should be described as modern.

There is, accordingly, nothing implausible about either conception as a way of characterizing the most recent epoch of human experience. Nor is there anything implausible about using both to describe the same period of time. These two conceptions of the modern age are not mutually exclusive. The same period of time may be consistently identified with both a sharp disruption of historical continuity and with the prominence of distinctively modern ideas and practices that arise after that discontinuity, as, for example, in those parts of the world where distinctively modern ways were introduced by means of conquest and colonialism.

But since these two ways of talking about the modern age employ the same vocabulary and that vocabulary has received relatively little critical scrutiny, it is easy to conflate them into one implausible claim: that *everything* after the modern divide is characterized in some important way by distinctly modern ideas and practices. It is especially easy to conflate the temporal and substantive conceptions of the modern age when, as we so often do, we identify the origins of the modern age with the Enlightenment and its attempts to break with past constraints on moral and scientific reasoning. For then we identify the disruption of historical continuity, after which things can never be the same again, with a self-conscious effort to break with the past and make sure that things never will be the same again. And it becomes very tempting to read the effects of this effort to break with the past into everything that happens after it first emerges to prominence.

In order to resist this temptation we need to think more precisely about the relationship between distinctly modern ideas and practices and the epoch which we characterize with reference to them. What makes them so significant that we have become accustomed to identifying our epoch with their rise to prominence? And what is the relationship between what is distinctly modern in the modern age and what is not? The tendency to conflate the substantive and temporal conceptions of the modern age makes it difficult to pose and answer these questions. But until we do, we will continue to be tempted to treat modernity as a coherent and integrated whole.

What's Modern and What's Not in the Modern Age?

It is relatively easy to answer this question when we are dealing with the temporal conception of the modern age. For in that case the modern is whatever is new, that is, anything that develops after the disruption of historical continuity that marks the beginning of the modern age. An idea or an institution is modern if it emerges after that divide; it is not if it appears before this disruption took place. For example, nationalism is a distinctly modern phenomenon, according to the temporal conception of the modern age, if it emerged for the first time in recent centuries; it is not modern if it is rooted in a kind of ethnocentrism that has been prominent throughout human history. Locating what's modern in the modern age in this way is a relatively straightforward, if often controversial, task. The more difficult problem is gaining some agreement about where to locate the point of discontinuity in historical development that begins the modern age.

It is considerably more difficult to distinguish what's modern from what's not when we are using the substantive conception of the modern age. For then it is no longer simply a matter of identifying new developments. We must instead pick out from among new developments those that share the special qualities we associate with distinctly modern ideas and practices. Nationalism, for example, may indeed be a new development and thus a modern phenomenon in the temporal sense. But it is not modern in the substantive sense unless it shares certain features of distinctly modern ideas and institutions, for example, that it supports in some way the industrial or capitalist forms of development that many thinkers associate with modernity. If it does not share such features, then nationalism may be a new, but not distinctly modern phenomenon, as I shall argue in Chapter 2. To locate the modern, according to the substantive conception of the modern age, we have to decide which of the many new elements in our social experience lead us to think that our social condition is qualitatively different from any that has gone before.

Which of the new developments that loom so large in our experience—the growth of technology, urbanization, mass media, industrialism, capitalism, globalization, nationalism, modernism, liberalism, egalitarianism, totalitarianism, and so on—make us think of ourselves as substantively modern? One might be tempted to answer this question by saying that the distinctly modern condition is the sum of all of these new and striking developments. But to answer the question in this way is to conflate the temporal and substantive conceptions of the modern age. It makes perfect sense, according to the temporal conception, to describe the modern age as the age of liberalism *and* totalitarianism, of capitalism *and* communism, of technocracy *and* egalitarianism, since the temporal conception makes no claim about the coherence or consistency of modern developments. But the substantive conception identifies the modern age as the period in which a core of distinctive ideas and practices rise to prominence and transform the character of our lives. All of these phenomena cannot be modern, according to this conception, unless behind their apparent opposition they all share some distinctively modern trait.

What then is the special quality of distinctly modern ideas and practice and why do we tend to treat its rise to prominence as epoch-making? The broad and varied ways in which we talk about the modern makes it difficult to offer a simple answer to these questions. I shall begin by distinguishing four ways in which the special quality of modern life has been described. Call them the philosophic, sociological, political, and aesthetic conceptions of modernity.

The philosophic conception associates modernity with the self-conscious break with tradition and received authority initiated by, among others, Bacon, Descartes, and the philosophers of the Enlightenment. The distinctive quality of modern ideas and practices, from this point of view, is an attitude that Hans Blumenberg has aptly described as "the self-assertion of reason." This "new quality of consciousness" urges us to master nature through rational analysis and reconstruction, rather than passively contemplate its order and beauty.[15] Modernity, in this conception, comes to be seen as a "project," a collective effort to transform the human condition by developing new and more effective ways of generating, gathering, and disseminating useful knowledge.[16] It involves both a conscious break with traditional authority and the assertion of control over the external environment by means of the development of scientific and technological knowledge. It is widely perceived as an epoch-making change of attitude for a number of reasons, including its success in discrediting religious traditions as a basis for philosophizing and the unprecedented power of the new sciences, which it helped create, to transform the material conditions of human existence.

The sociological conception of modernity starts with changing conditions and relations of social existence, rather than with changing ideas.[17] It focuses its attention primarily on the new forms of association created by capitalism and industrial society and the break with traditional authorities and customs that they have introduced.[18] Among the many distinctive qualities attributed to these forms of association are the rationalization of traditional authority studied by Weber and the unprecedented dynamism, the "constant revolutionizing of production, uninterrupted disturbance . . . everlasting uncertainty and agitation," that so fascinated Marx.[19] These qualities are widely viewed as epoch-making because they are seen as introducing a break with the traditional forms of association that have until now governed human life, rather than with a simple change from one tradition to another. As a result, modernity is opposed to tradition in the sociological conception, rather than to antiquity or the Catholic Middle Ages, as in the philosophic conception.

The political conception of modernity focuses its attention on the replacement of religious and aristocratic political hierarchies with more egalitarian and democratic forms of political legitimacy. The great symbol of political modernity is the French Revolution, the point at which many scholars locate "the birth of modernity."[20] The new, more democratic forms of political legitimacy introduced by the Revolution are generally perceived as epoch-making because of their ultimate success in eliminating aristocratic forms of political hierarchy. As Hegel suggested, all are free (at least in principle) in the modern age, while only some were free in its predecessors. Moreover, they are epoch-making because, as Tocqueville argued at length in *Democracy in America*, this shift from aristocratic to more democratic regimes has profound and pervasive effects on all aspects of modern ideas and institutions, from art and philosophy to manners and the family. Accordingly, modernity is opposed to aristocracy and theocracy in the political conception.

The aesthetic conception associates modernity with certain styles in art and literature, styles that begin to emerge in the last half of the nineteenth century and are commonly described as modernism. Baudelaire's celebration of modernity as the special quality of those new works of art that seek beauty and meaning in the ephemeral, in the constantly shifting conditions of modern existence, rather than in eternal forms, is the classic statement of this conception.[21] It is harder to say why the emergence of modernist styles should be perceived as epoch-making, except to the extent that one identifies new epochs in history with new epochs in aesthetics.[22] In the aesthetic conception modernity is opposed to the aesthetic orthodoxy of the time, be it classicism, romanticism, historicism, impressionism, or whatever.[23]

These four ways of characterizing modernity focus our attention in different directions: toward ideas, social conditions, perceptions of political legitimacy, and aesthetic styles. And they locate the birth of modernity in very different periods: in the seventeenth century for the philosophic conception, the late eighteenth century for the sociological and political conceptions, and the late nineteenth century for the aesthetic conception. Moreover, they are not completely consistent with each other. The aesthetic conception of modernity, for example, is in large measure a rebellion against the kind of ideas and practices associated with the philosophical, sociological, and especially the political conception of modernity. Modernism as an aesthetic movement was often associated with an effort to disrupt the "bourgeois modernity" sustained by liberal democratic institutions.[24]

Nevertheless, there is something that all four of these conceptions of modernity have in common: a focus on breaking with traditional authority and the accelerated and unprecedented rate of change that such activity brings about. In the philosophic conception this break with traditional authority is undertaken intentionally as a way of setting humankind on a new path. In the sociological conception it is a striking feature of everyday life, exemplified by both the secularization of public authority and the constant revolutionizing of the material conditions of life introduced by industrial production and modern technology. In the political conception it is an unavoidable fact of life in a political system in which inherited hierarchy no longer legitimates political authority. In the aesthetic conception of modernity the break with traditional authority is exemplified by the avant-garde artist's perpetual self-invention and rejection of received forms.

Accordingly, I would suggest that the distinctive substantive quality of modern ideas and practices is their emphasis on innovation and continual challenge to traditional authority. We describe these ideas and practices as modern not just because they emerge during the most recent period of history but also because they promote a continuing activity of "modernizing" or breaking with the past. "What is truly unique" about them is that they promote what might be called a permanent revolution in our life and thought, rather than a single break "where innovation occurs only at the beginning."

> The break at the beginning of the modern age embodied a *principle* of innovation in itself which made its constant further occurrence mandatory. As a consequence, the relation of each phase to its own preceding past—itself a phase of the revolution—remained that of critique and overcoming for the sake of further advance. . . . It made the revolution permanent, irrespective of whether its agents were still revolutionaries.[25]

This permanent revolution in modern lives is most evident in scientific research and in the ceaseless technological and commercial innovations of industrial society. It is far less evident, I shall argue in Chapter 4 ("What's Modern and What's Not in Liberal Democracy?"), in contemporary political life, which is why I believe that the modernity of modern politics has been greatly exaggerated. And while it certainly has played a powerful role in modern art, that role seems to be waning today with the increasing prominence of postmodernist forms of expression.

The "modern condition," the distinctive condition experienced by individuals who live in the modern age, refers to the life and experience of those who live with the consequences of the unprecedented dynamism introduced by distinctly modern ideas and practices. Living with these ideas and practices means living in an environment disrupted by attacks on traditional authority and the accelerated pace of change that they have introduced. It also means living with the influence of the many forms of life and thought that either resist or are indifferent to the unprecedented dynamism introduced by distinctly modern ideas and practices. Older, more traditional patterns of thought and association, as well as new developments that do not seek to challenge tradition in a characteristically modern way, thus coexist with distinctly modern ideas and practices in the modern age.

This mix of distinctly modern and nonmodern ideas and practices guarantees a large degree of incoherence in the life of modern individuals. Even the most modern of modern societies display, as Ernest Gellner has suggested, some of the incoherence of a badly decorated modern apartment in which "the plumbing, lighting and structure" are all high-tech but "the furnishing and decoration is strictly period."[26] The physical appearance and material infrastructure of these societies all point to the influence of distinctly modern ideas and modes of organization. But the political and cultural life that adorns and legitimates these structures is a confusing mélange of constitutional antiques, traditional forms, and modernist gestures. Looking only at the physical structures and economic capacities of such societies we might conclude that they are all of a modern piece. But when we look more closely we find a deeper incoherence. Continuities with the past play as large—or even a larger—role in maintaining the political and cultural practices of these societies as distinctly modernist impulses, a point that seems especially striking when one looks at the role of constitutionalism and the rule of law in liberal democratic politics, as I shall do in Chapter 4.

As Gellner notes, most social theorists are "somewhat contemptuous of the underlying incoherence" of such a picture of modern society.[27] Some, like Habermas, treat this incoherence as a sign that modernity is not yet complete. The completed project of modernity, Habermas argues, would create an ordered world in which science, politics, and art would each be practiced according to their own autonomous but complementary principles.[28] Others, like many of Habermas's postmodernist opponents, view this incoherence as a sign of modernity's imminent collapse. They are confident that "modernity, as a sociocultural entity, [is] disintegrating."[29] But this contempt for the possibility that the most distinctly modern practices and institutions flourish alongside distinctly nonmodern counterparts merely reflects an initial and, to my mind, unreasonable expectation that modernity should form a coherent and integrated whole in the first place.

And a Juggernaut Runs through It

Because of its unprecedented and largely uncontrollable dynamism, modernity is often portrayed as a juggernaut, as

> a runaway engine of enormous power which, collectively as human beings, we can ride to some extent but which also threatens to rush out of our control and which can rend itself asunder. The juggernaut crushes those who resist it, and while it sometimes seems to have a steady path, there are times when it veers away erratically in directions we cannot foresee. The ride is by no means wholly unpleasant or unrewarding; it can often be exhilarating and charged with hopeful anticipation. But, so long as the institutions of modernity endure, we shall never be able to control completely either the path or the pace of the journey. In turn, we shall never be able to feel entirely secure, because the terrain across which it runs is fraught with risks of high consequence.[30]

As Anthony Giddens notes in this invocation of the juggernaut image, the English term owes its origin to a Hindu procession in which an idol of Krishna as "lord of the world *(Jagannath)*" was dragged through the streets on a huge car beneath whose wheels the god's most devoted followers were often crushed. This image wonderfully captures the erratic motion and disruptive effects of the dynamism introduced into our lives by distinctly modern ideas and practices. Like a juggernaut, they cut a swath through familiar traditions and practices. And like a juggernaut, they often crush their most devoted adherents in the upheaval that they create.

But it is important when considering such images to remember that the modern age is more than the sum of the effects of distinctly modern ideas and practices. It is the period of time *within* which the juggernaut runs; it is not the juggernaut itself. The modern age, and the modern condition that develops within it, includes both the path ripped open by the juggernaut for distinctly modern ideas and practices and the vast territory that surrounds that path. When we think of modernity itself as the juggernaut, we tend to think of ourselves as riding or being dragged along inexorably by the dynamism of distinctly modern ideas and practices, like willing or unwilling passengers on a speeding train. But while we often occupy this position in the modern age, I would suggest that we just as often occupy the position of spectators, appalled or amused as we watch the juggernaut roll along, and then return to lives that are partly lived in the distinctly nonmodern terrain left intact on either side of the swath it has cut.

A river runs through traditional society, at least as we nostalgically recall it in the modern world. It sparkles and refreshes the senses while providing us with daily reassurance of nature's regularity. Not so the landscape of modernity. It heaves and shudders with incessant and irregular motion. It shakes with jackhammers and crackles with advertising—and a juggernaut runs through it.

Viewed in this way, modernity retains many of its most exhilarating and terrifying features. But it makes a considerable difference to our assessment of that condition if we think of ourselves as living alongside rather than astride the modern juggernaut. Astride the juggernaut we are driven, without choice or alternative, in whatever unintended direction the dynamism of distinctively modern ideas and practices takes us. Alongside the juggernaut we have the opportunity to balance its effects on our lives with the whole range of nonmodern ideas and practices that survive the swath that it has cut through our world.

Viewed as a coherent and integrated whole, modernity weighs down on us like some huge boulder. It seems to offer us nothing but the unhappy choice between leading miserable, flattened lives or escaping into romantic illusions about the past or future. But once we abandon the fetishism of modernities and the image of modernity as a coherent and integrated whole, we recover considerable room for maneuver and flexibility in our lives. For, as Robert Musil has suggested:

> If it turns out that our innermost being does not dangle from the puppet strings of some hobgoblin of fate, but on the contrary that we are draped with a multitude of small haphazardly linked weights, then we ourselves can tip the scales.[31]

Of course, *pace* Musil, many of our historical burdens are quite enormous, especially those associated with the changes introduced by distinctly modern ideas and practices. But Musil is right to suggest that history weighs us down with numerous "haphazardly linked weights" rather than with one enormous single burden. By balancing these weights in different ways, we can "tip the scales" in the direction of new and somewhat more satisfying forms of life, even if we cannot rise free of the weight of modern achievements and burdens.

Two

From the Moderns
to Modernity

Lucky the man who can say "when," "before," and "after"!
Terrible things may have happened to him, he may
have writhed in pain, but as soon as he can tell what
happened in chronological order, he feels as contented as
if the sun were warming his belly.

Robert Musil, *The Man Without Qualities*

The contrast between ancients and moderns goes back
at least as far as the fifth century. Indeed, the famous
seventeenth-century *querelle* was only the latest in a long
line of quarrels between ancients and moderns, a line
stretching back deep into the Middle Ages.[1] Modernity,
and especially the idea of the modern condition as a coherent and integrated whole, is, in contrast, a relatively new
or temporally modern idea. As we have seen, it does not
appear until the nineteenth century.

What leads us from the idea of the moderns to the idea
of modernity? One might think that the rise of historicism, the increasing sensitivity to the historical context of
thought and action, would be sufficient to explain why intellectuals began to treat modernity as a coherent and integrated whole.[2] But sensitivity to historical context takes a
variety of forms, many of which discourage us from dividing up human experience into coherent epochs. For Herder
and Spengler, for example, the decisive historical context of

41

thought and action is the life cycle of national cultures or world civilizations rather than broad temporal categories like antiquity and modernity. For many partisans of progress and social evolution, historical change is incremental and cumulative, so that explaining thought and behavior in terms of discrete epochs misrepresents the influence of historical context on our lives. And for many careful students of history, close attention to historical context reveals a variety of competing and crosscutting frameworks in every place or time rather than a single coherent context such as antiquity or modernity.

To get from the moderns to modernity thus calls for a particular form of historicism, one that views human development as a single story that unfolds in internally coherent epochal chapters. And it requires a form of historicism that relies heavily on comparisons between these epochs for its insights into the human condition. In this chapter I deal with the two most important and influential forms of historical social thought that develop such an approach and thereby promote the treatment of modernity as a coherent and integrated whole.

The first of these two forms of historical social thought is the intellectual tradition that I characterize in my book *The Longing for Total Revolution* as "left Kantianism." It is a tradition of philosophic social criticism begun by Fichte, Schiller, Schelling, and the young Hegel and carried on by many others, including the left Hegelians, Marx, Nietzsche, and many members of the Frankfurt school.[3] The second is what has come to be known as the "classical" tradition in social theory, an approach to the study of human relations inaugurated in the late nineteenth century by Durkheim, Tönnies, and Weber, among others. When contemporary scholars and intellectuals speak of modernity as a coherent and integrated whole, they most often draw on the language and insights of these two traditions of discourse.

These two intellectual traditions share a belief in the distinctive and unprecedented character of modern social life as well as a heavy reliance on epochal comparisons—with antiquity, in the case of left Kantianism, with models of traditional society, in the case of social theory. They differ in a variety of ways, perhaps most importantly in their incentives for constructing these comparisons. The left Kantians' interest in these comparisons is primarily diagnostic. Like Nietzsche, they are all "doctors of sick cultures." They want to figure out precisely what's wrong with us moderns and, they hope, how to cure it. The classic social theorists, in contrast, display a more explanatory interest in modernity.[4] They seek to figure out what keeps modern society together and functioning so effectively when, according to traditional wisdom, it should collapse into an anarchic war of all against all.[5] Each of these interests, I shall argue, leads the two groups to construct models of modernity that tend to exaggerate the coherence and integrity of modern life.

By returning to the end of the eighteenth century in order to explain the move from the moderns to modernity we are, it should be noted, moving back to a period of time prior to the emergence of the term modernity as a synonym for the modern condition. But we must not let this fact mislead us about the origins of the idea of modernity as an integrated and coherent whole. We need to keep in mind what Hegel has taught us, and the practitioners of *Begriffsgeschichte* sometimes forget, that the owl of self-consciousness flies only at dusk.[6] In other words, the explicit recognition of a concept in ordinary language most often points to the end, rather than the beginning, of any cultural development.

The Cultural Diagnoses of the Kantian Left

Hans Blumenberg suggests that the real strength of the modern self-assertion of reason lies in "the daily confirmation and life-worldly success of its method." In other words, what makes the modern rebellion against received opinion and traditional authority convincing is the external confirmation it receives by being able to identify and manipulate some of the forces that govern our everyday lives. Its corresponding weakness, Blumenberg adds, lies in the "uncertainty about what 'totality' this continuing success could ever bring forth."[7] Because modern self-assertion gains confirmation through the continual transformation of the external world, its successes are bound to undermine our sense of the world as a harmonious whole. If, as I suggested at the end of the last chapter, a juggernaut of unprecedented and previously unimaginable change runs through the landscape of modernity, a sense of division and disunity is bound to become prominent in the modern age.

This sense of division and disunity is the symptom with which left Kantian cultural diagnoses begin. As the young Hegel puts it in 1800, "the need for philosophy" emerges when "the might of union vanishes from the life of men."[8] "Everlastingly chained to a little fragment of the whole," writes Schiller,

> man himself develops into nothing but a fragment; everlastingly in his ear the monotonous sound of the wheel he turns, he never develops the harmony of his being, and instead of putting his stamp of his humanity upon his own nature, he becomes nothing more than the imprint of his occupation or of his knowledge.[9]

This famous lament about modern culture reverberates throughout nineteenth-century social criticism, from the young Marx's complaints about the division between private and public to Nietzsche's savage critique of modern civilization as a "handbook of inner culture for outward barbarians."[10] Schiller argues that while the division of human faculties has been a gain for the species, it has been a calamity for the individual. For the new spirit of culture produces useful knowledge only by dividing our lives into separate and opposing spheres of activity. The church fosters the spirit, the state protects the body. Labor becomes a private function performed in the service of self-preservation, rather than a communal activity. In short, the distinctively human qualities of reason and freedom become separated from the external forms of our life. And Kant's critical philosophy, the crowning achievement of modern culture for the first left Kantians, purports to demonstrate that this is the way things have to be, given the fundamental and inescapable dichotomies between duty and inclination, and between human freedom and natural necessity.[11]

Modernity emerges in left Kantian social criticism as a problematic condition, a consequence of the Enlightenment's one-sided assertion of human reason. Its dichotomies pervade every aspect of modern life and politics. They leave us dissatisfied with even our greatest achievements and frustrate our most concerted efforts to bring freedom into the world, as left Kantians argue in their analyses of the French Revolution.

Among the first generation of left Kantians were many disappointed partisans of the French Revolution in Germany at the end of the eighteenth century. Unlike Kant, they began by expressing unambiguous enthusiasm for the Revolution, commenting frequently on the parallels between Kant's Copernican revolution in philosophy and France's revolution in politics. (Fichte was the most enthusiastic in these comparisons. For him, one commentator has suggested, the execution of Louis XVI was the political equivalent of Kant's "liquidation of the thing-in-itself.")[12] The left Kantians tended to view the French Revolution through Kantian lenses and to interpret it as an attempt "to set law upon the throne, to honor man at last as an end in himself and to make true freedom the basis of political association."[13] As such, the Revolution emerges as the political completion of modern reason's rebellion against traditional authority. For "the work of blind forces possesses no authority before which freedom need bow." The Revolution, from this point of view, represents an effort to bring all claims to authority before "the tribunal of pure reason" and make "true freedom the basis of political association."[14]

(These words, like the majority of quotations I shall use to illustrate left Kantian opinions, come from Schiller's pen. I cite parallel passages from the works of Fichte, Schelling, Hölderlin, and the young Hegel in *The Longing for Total Revolution*. I quote primarily from Schiller's writings for three reasons. First of all, he is the first thinker to bring together all of the themes I identify with left Kantianism. Second, he provides an especially clear and influential account of the contrast between ancients and moderns. Finally, I cite him most because he writes so beautifully, and I am not above exploiting borrowed eloquence.)

For Schiller and the left Kantians, it is the dichotomous spirit of modern culture that doomed to failure the Revolution's attempt to make "true freedom the basis of political association." The revolutionaries seemed to believe that they could establish true political freedom simply by proclaiming its principles and destroying the arbitrary authority of the ancien régime. But, Schiller laments, the liberation they proclaimed found "a generation unprepared to receive it."[15] Educated by the Enlightenment to associate politics with autonomy, but socialized by everyday life in the old regime to associate political obligation with fear and self-interest, the French people became confused when the old regime fell. With their inclinations socialized in one direction and their sense of duty in another, they lacked a clear direction and began to oscillate between passive obedience and violently irrational assertions of collective will. Hence the Jacobin terror and the ultimate triumph of Napoleonic imperialism.

In the end, the revolutionaries failed, according to the left Kantians, because they assumed that, to use Marx's language, "political emancipation" could succeed without "human emancipation,"[16] that they could introduce free institutions without first creating free human beings. Without a "total revolution" in our "whole way of feeling,"[17] Schiller suggests, emancipation from arbitrary rule merely frees us to do our worst against each other. Freedom must become a component of human character, rather than just a principle of duty, if we are to make "true freedom the basis of political association." In other words, we need to heal the modern breach between duty and inclination, moral freedom and natural necessity, if the promise of the Revolution is ever to be fulfilled.

Of course, one might think that such a breach is unavoidable in any enlightened and civilized society. Certainly that is what Kant had argued. To counter this claim the left Kantians turned to the ancient Greeks. Greek life seems for them to defy the dichotomies between nature and freedom that Kant taught were inescapable. For them the Greek world lacks modernity's unfortunate "dividing wall between life and doctrine."[18] "Never for the Greek is nature purely physical nature, and for that reason he does not blush to honor it; never is reason for him purely reason, and thus he need not tremble in submitting to its rule."[19] These

comparisons with Greek culture convinced the left Kantians that cultural dichotomy is a distinctly modern disease
rather than an inescapable feature of the human condition.[20] As Schiller puts it in his famous essay *On Naive and
Sentimental Poetry,* the Greeks "are what we were; they are
what we shall become again . . . by means of our reason and
freedom."[21]

From this point of view modernity emerges as the latest,
but not the final, stage of human development. It is the unhappy middle condition suspended in history between two
happier conditions: the naive harmony of the Greeks and
the self-conscious and freely willed harmony of some future
age. As such, modernity is something to be transcended,
not simply rejected, according to left Kantians from Schiller
and Hegel to Marx and Nietzsche. The left Kantians seek
to preserve modernity's greater self-consciousness and subjective freedom in the more harmonious society that will
be created by the "total revolution" in our "whole way of
feeling."

Nevertheless, it is the underlying spirit of modern society
that poses the primary obstacle to a satisfactory human
existence for the Kantian left. As a result of their influence,
the spirit of modern society becomes the greatest object
of indignation for intellectuals educated in the German
philosophic tradition. The spirit of modern society, it is said
again and again, deforms and dehumanizes individuals. It
turns us into bourgeois, Philistines, last men—nothings.[22]
One of the greatest indignities that modern society imposes
on us, from this point of view, is that it teaches us to think
that human beings cannot amount to anything more than
the small-minded and slavish creatures that we see around
us. There is considerable debate among left Kantians about
what defines the spirit of modern society—a dichotomous
culture, the mode of production, the historical sense, the

forgetting of Being. But all agree that we will never know truly human individuals until we reach beyond the dehumanizing spirit of modern social relations.

For the purposes of our inquiry into the fetishism of modernities, the most striking feature of left Kantian cultural diagnoses is the way in which the distinctively modern expands to fill the entire horizon of our experience. Modernity, in these arguments, is within us and around us; it shapes our sentiments and our social relations, our ideas and our institutions. Its distinctive spirit of social interaction pervades the modern era and turns our social experience into a coherent and integrated whole. Modernity thus becomes a totality for the first time in left Kantian arguments. It is, of course, a "negative totality," in that what integrates modern life is an experience of division and disunity. But it is a totality nonetheless.[23] You cannot explain or correct any feature of modern life, according to these arguments, unless you first identify and uproot the underlying spirit that informs the whole. That is one of the most important lessons that the left Kantians drew from the failure of the French Revolution.

We are so used to this way of talking that it is hard to see its novelty—or for that matter, its persistence among intellectuals who loudly decry the concept of totality. In order to appreciate its novelty it is worthwhile comparing the left Kantians' talk of ancient and modern to the parallel discussions in the famous "quarrel" of the ancients and moderns in seventeenth- and eighteenth-century French thought. The French quarrel was about the relative value of ancient versus modern cultural achievements. The primary issue was who provided the finest models in art, literature, and philosophy, the ancients or the moderns.[24] Left Kantian discourse, in contrast, is concerned with the relative quality of ancient versus modern *life*. The primary issue here concerns character and identity, not just which models to follow. The left Kantians invoke the ancients to figure out who we are and what makes us that way. As a result, their comparison between ancients and moderns leads them to identify an underlying spirit of association that informs—and deforms—all of modern life.

The way in which the spirit of ancient and modern society is identified in these comparisons all but guarantees that we will exaggerate the integrity and coherence of both ancient and modern experience. The starting point in these comparisons is the recognition of some striking and distinctive limitation of modern theory and practice, for example, a sense of deep division and fragmentation. The comparison with an earlier and admired epoch that lacks this limitation both sharpens our image of what is distinctly modern and helps us imagine what life would be like without this distinctly modern limitation. The spirit of the ancients is thus identified indirectly in these comparisons, by asking ourselves what it would be like to live without some important element of modern experience. Greek antiquity plays the role in these comparisons of what Samuel Huntington (in his critique of modernization theories) calls a "residual category."[25] What looks at first like a straightforward attempt to identify the distinctive elements of ancient Greek theory and practice reveals itself on closer examination to be a reaction to some disturbing feature of modern experience. As a result, these comparisons not only use a selective focus that exaggerates the coherence of ancient Greek life and thought, they select that focus on the basis of something striking about *modern*, rather than ancient, experience.

I could go on at some length about the mischief created by this use of "the ancients" as a residual category. Think of how often modern political theorists invoke "the ancients," when they are really talking about the Greeks of the classical era . . . or rather the Athenians of that period . . . well, actually, the Athenian philosophers . . . no, in fact they really mean Aristotle, since Plato is so radically opposed to so much of Athenian, let alone "ancient," theory and practice. And this kind of mischief is not restricted to the partisans of the ancients. It appears just as much among intellectuals, from Benjamin Constant and Fustel de Coulanges to Niklas Luhmann and Stephen Holmes, who seek to break the spell of the ancients by pointing to what, from the modern perspective, looks like the complete subordination of private to public life in the ancient polis.[26]

In contemporary political thought it is Leo Strauss who is most responsible for the popularity of the invocation of the ancients as a residual category. He lends "the ancients"—by whom he means ancient students of politics from Aristophanes and Plato to Lucretius and Cicero—a coherence and consensus that is hard to justify given the manifest disagreements between Plato and Aristotle, let alone Plato, Epicurus, and Tacitus. Strauss can at least offer a possible justification for attributing such coherence and consensus to "the moderns," since he explicitly identifies modernity with the project of modern political philosophy.[27] But there is no parallel ancient "project" that could even begin to make it plausible to think of succeeding generations of ancient thinkers as co-conspirators in an effort to create a new world.[28] In the end, what unifies the ancients into a coherent group for Strauss is merely that they are *not* moderns, that they do not participate in the modern project of Enlightenment and the conquest of nature.

But I digress. My main point here is to show how left Kantian comparisons between ancients and moderns lead us to exaggerate the coherence of ancient and modern society. We have seen how antiquity's coherence is exaggerated by these comparisons. Let us now see how the same thing happens with modernity.

The construction of antiquity as a residual category helps us imagine what life would be like without the distinctive limitations of modern experience. As a historical alternative, rather than an imaginary utopia, this image of antiquity reinforces the hopes that these limitations are not a permanent feature of the human condition. Since we were whole once, one need not immediately dismiss as utopian our dreams of becoming whole again—even if attaining wholeness at a higher level, "by means of our reason and freedom," is a daunting challenge.[29]

With such an image of antiquity in mind, we can now reverse the roles played by each category and make modernity the residual category, a category constructed by imagining the absence of some distinctively ancient quality of life and thought. We can now construct a new vision of modernity by imagining what it is like to live without that wonderful quality of wholeness and harmony that we discovered among the Greeks. By doing so, we come back to where we started: a focus on the distinctive limitations of modern theory and practice. But by means of the comparison with the ancients, that limitation has expanded to fill the whole horizon of modern experience as the spirit of modern society. The spirit of modern society now looms large as the obstacle to any partial improvement that falls short of a total revolution in our whole way of feeling. And modernity emerges as a negative totality, the integrated and coherent whole that frustrates our hopes for a truly human cultural and political life.[30]

This idea of modernity as a negative totality is spread by the successive waves of left Kantian speculation over the last two hundred years. The first of these waves crests in the 1790s with the arguments of Schiller, Fichte, and the young

Hegel, among others. The second of these waves breaks after Hegel's death when left Hegelian radicals, like Marx, return to the young Hegel's struggles to close the gap between reason and reality and effect the realization of philosophy in our everyday lives. The third wave of left Kantian criticism develops after World War I with the rediscovery of Marx's early writings on alienation and dehumanization and the development of the various approaches associated with Marxist humanism.[31] The earliest left Kantian critiques of the dehumanizing spirit of modern society have been revised, reversed, demystified, turned upside down and rightside up by subsequent generations of social critics. But diverse and lively as this tradition of social criticism has been, most of its practitioners take for granted that it makes sense to talk about modernity as a coherent and integrated whole. They disagree about the sources of the dehumanizing spirit of modern society; they do not doubt its existence. As a result, the construal of modernity as a negative totality has been spread by the most important and influential strands of radical social criticism since the end of the eighteenth century.

The Dichotomies of Modern Social Theory

Let me turn now to modern or, as it has come to be known, "classic" social theory, the works by Weber, Durkheim, Tönnies, and others that did so much to establish the current discipline of sociology. Its contribution to the fetishism of modernities is somewhat more indirect but just as important.

As many have noted, classic social theory is grounded in a series of familiar dichotomies: "status" vs. "contract," "community" vs. "society," "mechanical" vs. "organic solidarity," and so on.[32] These dichotomies generally distin-

guish forms of social interaction based on shared or inherited identity from those based on voluntary association,
impersonal interaction, and functional differentiation.

Tönnies, Durkheim, Weber, and others favor these
conceptual dichotomies mainly because of their interest in
making sense of the new and unprecedented forms of social
order that they see emerging in the nineteenth century.
Communitarians of the left (Rousseau and the socialists)
and right (Burke, de Maistre, Bonald, etc.) had long argued,
like their contemporary followers, that the increasing individualism of modern theory and practice is threatening the
very possibility of a decent social order. The classic modern
social theorists suggest, instead, that what is happening in
the nations of Western Europe and North America is the
passing of familiar, traditional forms of social order into
new and unfamiliar forms of association. The main task
that they set out for themselves is to identify and explain
these new forms and sources of social order. Tönnies' concept of *Gesellschaft,* Durkheim's concept of "organic solidarity," Weber's concept of rationalization, even Marx's
concept of the capitalist mode of production, are all inspired, in large part, by the need to identify and explain the
unprecedented forms of social order that seem to develop
in a modern, increasingly individualistic world. The great
conceptual dichotomies upon which they build their social
theories thus represent, more than anything else, an attempt
to distinguish a novel modern form of social order from its
predecessors. Given sociology's debt to these dichotomies,
the very idea of "a sociology of modernity seems tautological at best." For, as Peter Wagner puts it, "what else is
sociology, if not the systematic attempt to come to an understanding of modern society?"[33]

These dichotomies parallel but do not exactly match the
dichotomy between modern and premodern epochs. They

represent ideal types of social order rather than periods of times. Characteristic features of each of these opposing types of social order can appear in the same epoch, even in the same set of actions. Weber, for one, was especially suspicious of epoch talk and the irrational "feeling of totality" that he believed inspires it.[34] He takes care to note, for example, that "no matter how calculating and hard-headed" our most instrumental relationships may be, they often develop "emotional values" more characteristic of communal than contractual bonds.[35] As a result, it should be clear that the use of classic social theory's dichotomies does not necessarily lead to a totalistic picture of modernity as an integrated and coherent whole.

Nevertheless, even Weber, one could argue, "developed a science of the modern world in spite of his own belief that the concept of an epoch was unscientific."[36] The dichotomies of classic social theory do not themselves represent epoch categories, but they are clearly inspired by the sense that human societies have been moving in the direction of one kind of social order and away from the other, a process that in the twentieth century comes to be known as modernization. This association with the modern epoch tends to broaden the claims of modern social theory in the hands of Weber's and Durkheim's successors. Because the modern type of social order generally follows after the traditional type, it is easy to jump to the conclusion that everything new must in some way be distinctively modern. As a result, what may have begun as an ideal type of new and distinctively modern forms of association soon turned into an ideal type of the modern condition, a model that helps us see how all of the leading developments of the modern age fit together into a coherent whole informed by distinctly modern ideas and practice. Because contemporary social theorists, such as Niklas Luhmann,[37] so often make increasing functional differentiation the key to this new condition, their treatment of modern society as a coherent and integrated whole is sometimes very hard to see. But, as I emphasized in the Introduction, one does not have to insist upon uniformity and harmony in order to treat modernity as a coherent and integrated whole. It is quite sufficient to point to a single principle of differentiation and conflict as the key to all the new developments in modern life and thought.

In twentieth-century modernization theory, modernity clearly emerges once again as a coherent and integrated whole, this time in contrast to tradition or traditional society.[38] Modernization theories tend to treat advanced Western industrial societies as the completion of a process of social evolution, or at the very least as a stable equilibrium point in that process. Accordingly, they assume that all of the new features of these societies fit together into a single coherent model of social organization. Modernity, in these theories, represents one side of a dichotomy rather than, as with left Kantian social criticism, the unhappy middle condition between a past and a future ideal.

Nevertheless, modernization theorists, like the left Kantians, rely on a "residual category"—"tradition" or "traditional society" in this case rather than antiquity—to render diverse modern ideas and practices coherent.[39] They too start by taking note of new and distinctive features of modern social life, such as increasing social differentiation, individualism, rationalization, and the disenchantment of nature. They then bring these distinctive features of modern society into relief by constructing a model of what life would be like without these distinctively modern phenomena. Doing so often leads them to exaggerate the degree of social homogeneity, consensus, and altruism in their accounts of premodern societies.[40] As Oscar Lewis has pointed out, no feuds are more persistent and bitter than disputes over land in a small peasant village.[41] The greater proximity of neighbors in a face-to-face society increases the intensity of conflicts as well as the possibilities for cooperation. Without anonymity and impersonality, there is no place to hide and let conflicts cool down. But the distinctive conflicts and diversity of premodern societies disappear from view when they are reconstructed as the negation of certain characteristic features of modern life.[42] And, as in left Kantian arguments, the exaggeration of the coherence of premodern society leads to the exaggeration of the coherence and integrity of modern society, at least as it is reconstructed in the imagination as a kind of society that lacks the consensus and irrationality that is written into the concept of traditional society.

Modernization theory no longer dominates the social sciences in the United States, as it did throughout the 1950s and 1960s.[43] But, like critiques of the dehumanizing spirit of modern society, it has popularized a way of speaking about modernity as a coherent and integrated whole. Oddly enough, just as that way of speaking began to die out in the 1970s and 1980s among social scientists, it has been taken up by many of modernization theory's most vehement opponents in the humanities.

Moreover, there is still a powerful tendency to think of modernity as a coherent and integrated whole among many contemporary social theorists, even when they reject the excesses of modernization theory. The dichotomies built into modern social theory still encourage them to analyze social phenomena by placing them on one side or the other of the modern/premodern divide, even if they completely reject the idea of modernity as the terminus or equilibrium point in social evolution.

In particular, these dichotomies encourage contemporary social theorists to characterize as modern any and all departures from older, traditional models of behavior, thereby losing sight of any distinction between the new and the modern. If a social phenomenon is new, from this point of view, then it must be modern, part of "the sum of enablements and constraints" created by modern societies.[44] This way of thinking clearly conflates the temporal and substantive conceptions of the modern age, for it interprets every development that emerges after a certain point in time as if it possessed some distinctly modern quality.

Consider, in this light, the debate among contemporary social theorists about the modernity of nationalism and the nation state. The opposing sides in this debate are most often described as "modernists" and "primordialists."[45] The modernists treat the nation as a fundamentally new form of political community, one that serves primarily as a means of supporting some characteristically modern set of practices, such as industrial society or the capitalist mode of production, and only incidentally as a way of expressing a community's cultural inheritance.[46] The primordialists, in contrast, insist that the nation gives voice to older, ethnocultural identities, identities that often overwhelm the goals of characteristically modern forms of association.

Missing in this debate is a third and, to my mind, much more sensible position: that the nation is indeed a new form of political association, but not a distinctly modern one. Such a position would allow one to account both for the obvious novelties that nationalism has introduced into communal life and for the fact that nationalism works to undermine characteristically modern forms of association as often as it works to support them. But the widespread conflation of the temporal and substantive conceptions of modernity make it very difficult to formulate such a position. Treating modernity as a coherent and integrated whole makes it appear that every new development must serve in some way to sustain characteristically modern practices and institutions. And it makes it appear that anything that serves to undermine modern practices and institutions must represent an inheritance from the premodern past—unless, of course, it is a harbinger of the postmodern future.

Modernity and the Holocaust

When we conflate the new with the modern in this way, we tend to suppress the unexpected and shocking features of new developments in favor of an emphasis on characteristics drawn from already familiar models of modernity. Take the continuing debate about the "modernity" of the Holocaust. Initially, most critics tended to treat Nazi genocide, and Fascism in general, as something like the return of the repressed, an outbreak of the primitive, barbaric passions that modern society was designed to keep under control. Later on, however, students of the Nazi regime began to emphasize the distinctly modern elements of the Holocaust, especially its heavy reliance on modern technological and organizational achievements. The most familiar version of the modernist interpretation of the Holocaust is Hannah Arendt's famous argument about the "banality of evil," her insistence that it was bureaucratic rationality pushed to its logical extreme, rather than an outbreak of barbaric passions, that was most responsible for the Holocaust.[47]

Zygmunt Baumann develops such an interpretation at length in his influential study *Modernity and the Holocaust.* "The holocaust," he argues, "is a byproduct of the modern drive to a fully designed and fully controlled world." It is "a legitimate resident in the house of modernity; indeed one that would not be at home in any other house."[48]

In the end, however, Baumann's argument for this position amounts to little more than the claim that modern ideas and modes of organization are "necessary conditions" for the Holocaust, the assertion that without certain modern innovations "the holocaust would be unthinkable."[49] But the same is true of traditional anti-Semitism and numerous other nonmodern developments without which the Holocaust would be unthinkable.[50] It is only his implicit assumption that modernity forms a coherent and integrated whole that allows Baumann to conclude that the Holocaust is especially "at home" in modernity rather than in some of the other times and places associated with its other necessary conditions. (Indeed, it is only this assumption that allows him to describe modernity as a "home" in the first place.) Only then would the mere employment of modern bureaucracy and technology make an event like the Holocaust "a legitimate resident in the house of modernity," regardless of all the other non- or anti-modern conditions without which it would be unthinkable.[51]

If one is speaking of modernity in the temporal sense, then it makes sense to say that the Holocaust is at home only in modernity. For it is only in the modern epoch that all of the conditions that made the Holocaust possible have come together. But if one is speaking of modernity in the substantive sense, as I believe Baumann is, then it makes little sense to describe the Holocaust in this way. For then, as we have seen, distinctly modern forms of technology and social organization merely contribute to the Holocaust, although perhaps in ways that have received too little attention up to now. But by conflating the temporal and substantive senses of modernity one can speak as if the Holocaust is *nothing but* "a byproduct of the modern drive to a fully designed and fully controlled world."[52] For then one can identify the distinctly modern ideas and practices that make some contribution to the Holocaust with the epoch that contains all of the conditions, distinctly modern or not, that made the Holocaust possible.

If our only two choices were modern or premodern, then it might make sense to ask whether the Holocaust was an outbreak of premodern barbarism or the "extreme exemplification of organized modernity."[53] But in this debate about the modernity of the Holocaust—as in the debates about the modernity of the nation-state—the possibility of new but not necessarily modern developments disappears from view. The fetishism of modernities encourages us to characterize things as either modern or premodern. If the Holocaust is not a continuation of traditional forms of group persecution, then it must be an integral part of modernity, according to this way of thinking.

I agree that it makes sense to describe the Holocaust as a new and unprecedented form of group persecution. But I do not think that distinctively modern forms of technology and bureaucratic organization provide sufficient explanations for its occurrence. The Holocaust, I would suggest, is an example of something new but not distinctively modern in the modern age. There may be many other such surprises in store for us, surprises that we could not predict simply by considering the consequences of distinctly modern ideas and practices.

Ironically, arguments of this sort about the modernity of the Holocaust end up obscuring the very feature of recent political developments that their advocates insist upon so vigorously: their novelty. By characterizing such developments as modern, these arguments encourage us to use the familiar practices and institutions associated with models of modern society to make sense of unexpected political ideas and institutions. The dangers posed by terrible events like the Holocaust can then be assimilated to the already familiar dangers associated with instrumental rationality, bureaucratic organization, and other characteristically modern attitudes and institutions. In this way, these arguments make the possibility of surprises from new and unfamiliar developments disappear from view.

In a strange way, talk about the modernity of the Holocaust is reassuring. It may be frightening to realize that familiar features of our society, like bureaucracy and technological research, may bear the seeds of terrible violence and genocide. But unnerving as that prospect may be, at least we can be assured that we are not marching through some completely *uncharted* territory if such horrific acts can be explained in terms of familiar modern causes. In this way, the fetishism of modernities, even in its most ominous and critical forms, serves to diminish our fear of the unexpected.

"Lucky the man," writes Robert Musil in *The Man without Qualities,*

> who can say "when," "before," and "after"! Terrible things may have happened to him, he may have writhed in pain, but as soon as he can tell what happened in chronological order, he feels as contented as if the sun were warming his belly.[54]

By chronologically ordering the dangers in our experience, by placing them into familiar "modern" patterns, the fetishism of modernities provides us with this kind of contentment, even in the midst of often apocalyptic pronouncements about where we are heading. The price of this false comfort, however, is a certain blindness to the possibility of unexpected dangers and, more generally, an impoverishment of our experience, as we strive to force its novel and unexpected features into the familiar patterns of modern—and now, postmodern—society.

Hans Blumenberg suggests that the primary source of myth is the need to name the forces that threaten us and thereby limit the variety "of directions from which 'it can come at one.'" We would be paralyzed with fear if the whole horizon of our experience were equally threatening. As a result, we have a deep and abiding need to name and divide the powers that confront us. "Anxiety," Blumenberg argues, "must again and again be rationalized into fear, both in the history of mankind and in that of the individual."[55]

The fetishism of modernities names and divides the powers that history and social development throw at us, thereby rationalizing a generalized anxiety about where history is taking us into a recognizable fear. As such, it clearly serves as a myth in Blumenberg's sense, although one concerned with history rather than nature.[56] We probably cannot do without at least some myths of this sort, stories that allow us to divide up our historical experience into more or less threatening segments. Viewing history as a completely patternless flow of events probably would create paralysis and terror in most of us.[57] Nevertheless, that does not mean we should simply accept whatever myths and stories that come our way. It all depends on what we gain and lose from one way of constructing our historical experience or another. And as I suggested in the Introduction, treating modernity as a coherent and integrated whole has become a stale cliché that conceals more than it reveals, that impoverishes rather than enriches our experience of the world. It is time, I believe, to turn to some other story.

Three

Postmodernity: Figment of a Fetish

The sooner this nonsense stops, the better.

Ernest Gellner, *Postmodernism, Reason and Religion*

Although the title and epigraph of this chapter may sound rather polemical, I want to emphasize at the start that the object of my criticism here is the idea of postmodern*ity,* the idea of a distinctively postmodern social condition, rather than the set of theories, styles, and attitudes loosely characterized as postmodernism. As a result, readers expecting a slam-bang refutation of postmodern relativism may be disappointed by what I have to say in this chapter. While I would certainly not describe myself as a postmodernist, I am, as already noted, quite sympathetic to many ideas and attitudes associated with postmodernism.[1]

But I have little sympathy for the idea of postmodernity, for the notion that we have entered into some new, distinctively postmodern condition. Accordingly, one major purpose of this chapter will be to distinguish between the concepts of postmodernism and postmodernity. Usage offers little guidance here since contemporary intellectuals often employ these terms interchangeably.[2] Nevertheless, I believe that it is very important to distinguish between the two. You can subscribe to all kinds of postmodern ideas and still vehemently deny that we are entering a new social condition called postmodernity.[3] Indeed, I believe that postmodern convictions should make you deeply suspicious of such a claim. Conversely, you can believe that we are entering into a new postmodern age without subscribing to postmodern ideas at all. Accordingly, many conservative critics of postmodern relativism and multiculturalism have eagerly appropriated the idea of postmodernity.[4] For if modernity has ended in exhaustion and self-contradiction, then conservatives have reason to hope that the modern forces eroding traditional authorities and values have lost much of their potency.

The concept of postmodernity registers the impression that the emergence of postmodernism is a watershed between epochs. Like the concept of modernity, it tends to drift between temporal and substantive meanings so that its proponents often talk as if, after the postmodern divide, things will never be the same again because they will all become postmodern in some way. It is this kind of talk that has inspired the rush to discover the distinctly postmodern form of every contemporary phenomenon, from family ties to investment strategies. But this kind of talk is rooted in an illusion fostered by the lingering influence of the fetishism of modernities. I criticize this illusion, just as I criticized the fetishism of modernities itself, in order to get a better sense of what really has changed in our condition and what has not in the wake of the emergence of postmodern ideas and attitudes.

From Postmodernism to Postmodernity

Let me begin by stating my main objection to the idea of postmodernity as simply and directly as I can. It is only because so many intellectuals are accustomed to thinking in terms of the fetishism of modernities that they are inclined to treat recent changes in cultural and social life as the threshold to a new postmodern condition. If you think of modernity as an integrated and coherent whole, then new developments that depart from its familiar patterns might well suggest to you that modernity is "disintegrating."[5] Moreover, if you believe that what gives modernity its coherence and purpose is a particular set of beliefs about human emancipation and the conquest of nature, and you believe that "an epoch approaches its end when its fundamental conviction begins to weaken,"[6] then the popularity of postmodernist criticisms of these beliefs may well suggest to you that we have left modernity behind.

But if, as I have argued, this portrayal of modernity as an integrated and coherent whole is untenable, then the idea of postmodernity is also untenable, a mere figment of our modernity fetish. For if there is no reason to treat modernity as a coherent and integrated whole, there is no reason to treat departures from familiar modern patterns, such as the emergence of postmodern ideas and attitudes, as a sign of the disintegration of modernity. The modern juggernaut of technological progress and mass production has co-existed quite comfortably for some time now—since the beginning of the twentieth century, at least—with a high culture that treats it with a great deal of contempt. I believe that it can coexist just as well, perhaps even more comfortably, with a largely postmodern culture.

For this reason I conclude that the basic social conditions with which I identified modernity at the end of the first chapter have not changed. A juggernaut of material change and technological innovation still runs through our age, disrupting many of our most settled practices and authoritative traditions. What is changing is the set of cultural patterns that emerge on either side of the swath that this juggernaut cuts through our lives. Such changes are far from insignificant. But they leave intact what I consider to be the most important and distinctive features of the modern social condition.

That is my argument in a nutshell. But, of course, things never remain so simple with the current intellectual culture. For one thing, the most influential prophets of postmodernity would deny most of the assumptions I have attributed to them. Indeed, most of them explicitly deny that they are talking about anything like a postmodern age. Even Jean-François Lyotard, whose famous book, *The Postmodern Condition*, is more responsible than any other publication for the current interest in the idea of postmodernity, complains that he never meant to describe postmodernity as "a new age."[7] And the leading social theorist of postmodernity, Zygmunt Baumann, the author of *Intimations of Postmodernity* and numerous other books on the postmodern condition, insists that postmodernity is a new "state of mind" rather than a new epoch or social condition.[8]

I must admit that I find these disclaimers rather annoying. These theorists get everybody talking about the new postmodern age, searching high and low for the new postmodern version of everything under the sun, and then tell us to stop because they didn't really mean it after all! It would be easy to undermine these disclaimers by pointing out that Lyotard speaks frequently of "the postmodern age" and associates it with the transition to a postindustrial economy; or that Baumann frequently describes postmodernity as a "social condition," and as "a cohesive aggregate of a new type of society . . . a model of its own," and that he does so in the very same book in which he insists that postmodernity is only a state of mind.[9] But contradiction hunting is a tedious activity to read and write about. Instead, I would like to examine the source of the contradiction—or ambiguity, if you prefer—in the way in which these thinkers describe postmodernity. Why is it that they advance and then feel compelled to withdraw these suggestions about leaving modernity behind and crossing over into a new era? Once we answer that question we will be in a better position to understand why these disclaimers have been so remarkably ineffective in stifling speculation about the coming postmodern epoch. For these disclaimers, like rabbinic injunctions against speculating about when the Messiah will come, seem only to have deepened the current obsession with talking about the end of the modern epoch.

The source of this ambiguity in characterizing postmodernity lies, not surprisingly, in the ambiguity of the way in which we characterize modernity. The term modernity, as I noted in Chapter 1, is used to characterize both a distinctive quality of certain recent ideas and practices and the epoch in which this quality rises to prominence. Similarly, postmodernity is used to characterize both a distinctive quality of certain postmodern ideas and practices and the epoch in which they rise to prominence. Do these postmodern ideas and practices have anything like the potential to transform the basic conditions of our life that distinctively modern ideas and practices have had? If they do, then we might be justified in talking about the end of modernity and a new postmodern age. If not, then modernity, the epoch that we associate with distinctively modern ideas and practices, is still with us, since the transformations that they have wrought are still an important and prominent feature of our social landscape.

The characterization of postmodernity as a quality, in particular, as a quality of aesthetic experience, is the older and more familiar use of the term. Until the late 1970s postmodernism was treated almost exclusively as an aesthetic discourse. Discussions of postmodernism emphasized the waning of modernist styles in art and literature. In this discourse, *postmodernism* is the name for a new style that broke with the distinctive qualities celebrated by modernist aesthetics, and *postmodernity* is a name for the new aesthetic qualities, such as irony, multiple perspectives, conscious anachronism, and so on, that are beginning to replace modernism's favored aesthetic qualities in contemporary art, literature, and especially architecture.[10]

When we talk about postmodernity as an aesthetic quality, the modernity that we are leaving behind is a distinctive quality of modernist culture, *not* the modern epoch, *not* the social condition brought into the world by the Enlightenment, technology, and industrial society. Understood in this sense, postmodernism is a relatively unproblematic concept, comparable in form to concepts like Postimpressionism. For, in this sense, it simply refers to the new styles and tastes that have developed in reaction to modernism, which was the style that had dominated European high culture since the end of the nineteenth century until recent decades.

The conceptual problems with postmodernity begin when we extend postmodernism into philosophic and sociological discourse. For we then begin to conceive of the modernity that postmodernism leaves behind far more broadly as the philosophic and sociological conceptions of modernity come into play alongside the more limited aesthetic conception.[11] When modernity is conceived of as the quality that distinguishes modern thought since the scientific revolution or as the special quality of life in an advanced industrial society, postmodernism turns into the movement that succeeds the Enlightenment and the world it helped bring into being, rather than just the style that succeeds and reacts against modernism. And modernism also comes to be conceived far more broadly, as a way of characterizing all of the positions that advocate Enlightenment, industrial development, and human emancipation.

This broadening of the use of the term modernism creates considerable confusion in contemporary debates since aesthetic modernism so often expressed a reaction against these very beliefs in rationalism and progress that contemporary intellectuals tend to characterize as modernist. Many of the most influential modernists, such as T. S. Eliot or Ezra Pound, detested the modernity of equal rights and technological progress. Others, such as the futurists, were much more favorably disposed to technological innovations. But almost all modernists dismissed the liberal vision of human progress through Enlightenment as a mindless platitude.[12]

As long as postmodernism stuck to aesthetics and the waning of modernist styles, it made little sense to talk about the end of *modernity*. For, from this perspective, it was *modernism*, the aesthetic style that dominated high culture throughout most of the twentieth century, that was passing from the scene, not some broader social condition called modernity. It is only with the extension of postmodernist thinking into philosophy and sociology that postmodernism begins to be associated with claims about "the end of modernity."

If one thinks of modernity as an integrated and coherent whole, then it is relatively easy to extend postmodernism in this way. The disintegration of modernist culture will then suggest the disintegration of distinctively modern ideas and modes of social organization. Accustomed by Marx and his followers to treat culture as a reflection of our distinctive social condition, many contemporary cultural theorists assume that a shift in aesthetic styles must mean there has been a transformation of our basic social conditions, even if they no longer accept Marxian justifications for treating the two as a coherent and integrated whole. Of course, since there is no reason to rule out the possibility that the same social conditions could generate different cultural reflections, this inference is fallacious.[13] Nor is there any reason, once one gives up the characterization of modernity as an integrated and coherent whole, to expect that social and cultural conditions should reflect each other in any case. The current debate on postmodernism is often confined to the question of whether postmodernism represents, as Fredric Jameson puts it,[14] "the cultural logic of late capitalism" or a sign of the disintegration of the distinctively modern social conditions associated with capitalism and industrial society. But both sides in this debate seem to assume that culture and socioeconomic practices fit coherently together. They only disagree about which mode of social organization postmodern culture expresses.

The broadening of postmodernism began to take place in the late 1970s, the key work being Lyotard's *The Postmodern Condition*, which was published in 1979 and translated into English in 1984. Lyotard extends postmodernism into philosophy by pointing to affinities between the rejection of modernist aesthetics and the increasingly popular rejection of foundationalism and of philosophic theories of emancipation and historical progress. He argues that just as postmodernist critics can no longer take seriously modernist gestures of artistic autonomy and mastery of their materials, so contemporary philosophers can no longer take seriously the grand claims of intellectual autonomy and world mastery asserted by modern philosophers from Bacon and Descartes to Hegel and Marx. Like postmodern aesthetics, postmodern philosophy exhibits "incredulity toward metanarratives," the grand constructions of history as the conquest of nature or the progressive overcoming of alienation that modern philosophers use to legitimate their claims to knowledge. Similarly, Lyotard extends postmodernism into sociology by suggesting that there are important parallels between recent broadscale changes in social organization, such as the move in the direction of a post-industrial and information-based economy, and the qualities celebrated by postmodernist aesthetics. He argues that just as postmodern art and literature emphasize multiple perspectives and broken narratives, so the postindustrial world leaves us with a multiplicity of competing and incommensurable standards by which to measure the value of any knowledge claims. Lyotard's claim that we have entered into a "postmodern condition" rests on the strength of these parallels between changes in aesthetics, philosophy, and socioeconomic organization. For Lyotard we are on the threshold of a new epoch because all of these changes line up together and reinforce each other.

This is an extraordinarily suggestive claim, especially for many radical intellectuals, for whom an era truly has ended with the collapse of the revolutionary tradition that gave them much of their identity. Moreover, there is nothing that intellectuals of every stripe love better than the invention of a new epoch or paradigm. A new paradigm is always good for intellectual business, whether one is looking for a thesis topic or the subject for a potential best-seller, since it allows us to reopen every issue in order to fit old facts into new forms.

But it is also an immensely ambitious claim that is based, at best, on rather vague and tenuous evidence. There can be little doubt that postmodernity, the aesthetic quality celebrated by postmodernists, has arrived. It is all around us, in the buildings we work in, the books we read, the television we watch, the computer screens with which we interact. Irony, multiple perspectives, disjointed narratives, playful anachronisms—the characteristic gestures of postmodern culture stare back at us from almost every direction. But there can be a great deal of doubt about whether postmodernity, the new social condition, has arrived. It is thus understandable that, when pressed to defend themselves, the prophets of the postmodern condition rally to the much surer ground surrounding the description of postmodernity as a state of mind or stylistic quality. The ambiguity of the term as well as the fact that it was, like modernity, first used to describe an aesthetic quality, provides considerable cover for this retreat. Indeed, it hides the fact that a retreat has even taken place.

As a result, for all the outpouring of literature on postmodern thought, it is extremely rare "to find the ideas of postmodernism, postmodernity and the postmodern the object of philosophical attention at the level at which they are constituted, as periodizing concepts of cultural history."[15] But with the extension of postmodernism from aesthetics into philosophy and sociology, that is exactly what these concepts have become. That is why the most influential postmodernists have been writing books with titles like *The Postmodern Condition, Intimations of Postmodernity,* and *The End of Modernity,* rather than books with titles like "The Triumph of Postmodern Aesthetics," which is what we would expect if they took seriously their disdain about the epochal connotation of the term postmodernity.[16]

The basic insight of these books, once we get beyond their protective disclaimers, is that recent intellectual and cultural changes are epochmaking, that they represent the threshold of a fundamental transformation in the way we live. Like Albert Borgmann, author of *Crossing the Postmodern Divide,* the authors of these books seem to believe that "an epoch approaches its end when its fundamental conviction begins to weaken and no longer inspires enthusiasm among its advocates"[17]—although they would probably consider it very naive to say so. It would be much easier to defend such a claim if one limited the meaning of the word "epoch" in this statement to a state of mind or an aesthetic quality. But that would reduce the claim to a tautology: that an epoch in the history of human convictions (or states of mind) ends when widely held convictions lose their support. In other words, attitudes change when attitudes change. That is what would happen as well to claims about the end of modernity and the postmodern condition if we took seriously the disclaimers that they do not refer to epochmaking changes. In order to evaluate these claims and the epochal speculations they have inspired, we need to look carefully at postmodern narratives about the rise and fall of modernity, rather than at the ambiguous denials that any such story is being told.

Postmodern Narratives of Modernity

Lyotard is the author of the most influential of these narratives, even though he is best known for his defense of postmodernism as "incredulity" toward "grand narratives" about human history.[18] Although Lyotard disdains modern philosophers' attempts to legitimate their authority by invoking such narratives, he himself tells a story about our deliverance from the ravages caused by modern ideas about progress and human emancipation, a story that ends with a strident call to action:

> The nineteenth and twentieth centuries have given us as much terror as we can take. We have paid a high enough price for the nostalgia of the whole and the one, for the reconciliation of the concept and the sensible, of the transparent and the communicable experience. Under the general demand for slackening and for appeasement we can hear the mutterings of the desire for a return to terror, for the realization of the fantasy to seize reality. The answer is: Let us wage a war on totality; let us be

witnesses to the unpresentable; let us activate the differences and save the honor of the name.[19]

If this is not a grand narrative designed to legitimate a particular philosophic stance, then I do not know what is. Its appeal rests largely on our familiarity with arguments about the self-destruction of the modern drive for human emancipation and the conquest of nature, arguments made by philosophers and social theorists, such as Heidegger, Marcuse, Foucault, and Adorno, who never denied that they were in the business of devising grand historical counter-narratives.[20] But for now let us put aside the self-contradic-tion in Lyotard's position and look at the narrative itself.

One limitation of postmodern narratives about the self-destruction of modernity is their overly philosophic, or more precisely, overly epistemological characterization of the distinctive feature of modern ideas and practices. Here is a typical example. It is taken from *Enlightenment's Wake*, a book by the political theorist John Gray, a recent convert from Hayekian individualism to a kind of "postliberal-ism." Gray suggests that the modern period is "ruled" by the Enlightenment project, which, following Alisdair Mac-Intyre, he defines as the attempt to provide an "independent rational justification of morality." He then argues that "if, as I believe, the enlightenment project is self-destroying, then that signals the close of the modern period."[21]

If we think of modernity as a grand Cartesian project of self-grounding, then it would be hard to deny that modernity has run its course and destroyed itself, as Gray suggests. After all, none of us can pull ourselves out of the swamp by our own hair. From this point of view, Descartes is the paradigmatic modern thinker; Cartesian efforts to build a certain foundation for knowledge in the thinking self are the model for the Enlightenment project; and skepticism and "relativism" are modernity's most dangerous enemies.[22]

But this is a far too philosophic picture of the Enlightenment, let alone of the ruling ideas of "the modern period,"[23] as if the most important problem for modern thinkers was the invention of unshakable foundations for their arguments. What does one do, according to this point of view, with the great skeptics in Enlightenment thought, from Montaigne and Bayle to Montesquieu and Hume? These thinkers were not just friends, rather than enemies, of the Enlightenment; they were celebrated as great role models of enlightened thought.

If the Enlightenment project was a grand Cartesian effort at self-grounding, then it was a failure almost before it got started. For by the eighteenth century, Cartesian foundationalism received very little respect. Jean d'Alembert, for example, celebrates Descartes in the "Preliminary Discourse" to *The Encyclopedia* for his rebellious and doubting spirit rather than for his fruitless quest for certainty. "Descartes," writes d'Alembert, "showed intelligent minds how to throw off the yoke of scholasticism, of opinion, of authority." He apologizes for Descartes by suggesting that "if Descartes concluded by believing he could explain everything, he at least began by doubting everything, and the arms which we use to combat him belong to him no less because we turn them against him."[24]

Bacon, rather than Descartes, was the guiding spirit of *The Encyclopedia*, that great monument and icon of the Enlightenment.[25] It was Bacon's call for "a total reconstruction of sciences, arts, and all human knowledge" that the Encyclopedists answered.[26] *The Encyclopedia* was part of a vast collective effort at generating, gathering, and preserving useful knowledge, rather than a search for an "independent rational justification of morality." Like the universities, laboratories, and computer networks that are heirs to this effort, the *Encyclopedia* was a means of preserving useful knowledge from natural and social catastrophes so that the human race would never experience another "dark" age. If it is appropriate to describe the Enlightenment as a "project," then this was its goal. Ironically, when Lyotard states that despite "the decline of the 'project of modernity,' . . . there is not now, and never again will there be, a loss or diminution of knowledge and expertise,"[27] he is implicitly acknowledging the success of that project as Bacon and the Encyclopedists understood it.

How delighted Bacon and the Encyclopedists would have been with the computer, with its extraordinary potential for information storage, retrieval, and diffusion! And, as a result, how ridiculous it is to think of the changes in the direction of a postindustrial information society as a significant departure from the spirit of modernity.[28] These changes may be very significant indeed. But they follow, rather than depart from, distinctively modern ideas and practices.

Postmodernist narratives about modernity's rise and fall exaggerate the importance of Cartesian foundationalism because postmodernists tend to reconstruct modernity as a negative image of their own favored qualities. "Postmodern discourse generates its own concept of 'modernity,'" a concept that emphasizes the lack of all of those characteristics that are said to distinguish postmodernity.[29] If postmodernity is characterized by contextualism, relativism, and pluralism, then the distinguishing features of modernity will appear to be foundationalism and the ruthless quest for certainty. From this point of view, Zygmunt Baumann suggests, "relativism" is "the evil genius of [modern] European philosophy; anybody suspected of not fortifying doctrine against it tightly enough was brought to book and forced to defend himself against charges, the horrifying nature of which no one put in doubt."[30]

Here we see an almost paranoid exaggeration of modern thought's quest for certainty, as if Enlightenment thinkers spent their time conducting inquisitions, rather than hiding from them, or hunting and torturing skeptics like Montesquieu and Hume, rather than celebrating them. When we reconstruct the Enlightenment, let alone modernity, as what is *not* postmodern, I am afraid that something like this implausible picture is the result.[31] Numerous important things disappear from this picture of modernity, not the least of which is the indispensable role of skepticism and relativism in Enlightenment struggles against religious and traditional authority.

Modernity plays the role of "residual category" in many postmodern narratives that antiquity and traditional society play in left Kantian and modernization theories. Like antiquity and traditional society, its distinctive characteristics are identified indirectly, by negating distinctive features of contemporary theory and practice. Modernity is imagined in these postmodern narratives as a condition that lacks postmodernity's celebration of pluralism and relativism. As a result, it is imagined as a far more coherent and integrated—not to mention singlemindedly rationalist—condition than it appears to be when examined directly. In other words, because many postmodernists invoke modernity as a residual category, they become susceptible to the fetishism of modernities and begin to treat modernity as a totality, as a coherent and integrated whole. And because they tend to think of modernity as a coherent and integrated whole, they are tempted to treat departures from familiar modern models as a sign of the emergence of a new postmodern totality, complete with its own internal coherence. This is what leads them to treat all kinds of disconnected developments, such as the rise of postmodern culture and the emergence of information-based economies, as if they share a deep, modernity-transcending affinity.

By suggesting that many postmodern narratives treat modernity as a totality, I am courting considerable controversy, since engaging in totalizing discourse is one of the worst sins in the postmodernist catechism. How can postmodern narratives declare "war on totality" with one breath and then proceed to make prominent use of the concept in another? One reason is that the totality that Lyotard and others declare war on is what we might call "positive totality," the integration of life and experience into a harmonious and fully consistent whole, while the totality that he himself invokes in his analysis of modernity is a negative totality, a condition in which a prominent contradiction or division integrates the theory and practice of an epoch. This characterization of modernity as a negative totality plays a prominent role in radical thought from the young Hegel to Marcuse and persists even in the work of social critics like Adorno and Derrida, thinkers who express the most vehement opposition to the concept of totality.[32]

Moreover, we should also distinguish between what Martin Jay calls longitudinal and latitudinal totality.[33] Longitudinal totality integrates all of human experience, as in Hegelian accounts of history as the actualization of freedom or in Marxian accounts of the overcoming of alienation through social labor. Latitudinal totality, in contrast, integrates experience across one period of time or group of individuals as opposed to another. Its totalities are bounded, those of particular nations and epochs rather than of human experience as a whole. We might call latitudinal totality local as opposed to universal totality. Postmodern narratives are resolutely opposed to longitudinal totality but often make use of the latitudinal variety. Indeed, the contemporary revolt against the concept of totality is often conducted, as in Foucault's work, by noting the historical discontinuities that make one epoch's experience completely unlike another's.[34] As a result, postmodernists often emphasize the integrity and coherence of one epoch's experience in the midst of uncompromising attacks on the idea of totality itself.

Foucault is especially responsible for this way of thinking. The coherence that he assumes within periods is a key assumption that allows Foucauldians to imitate the master. As a visiting philosopher—a full-time philosopher of science and only a part-time Foucauldian—once announced at a lecture I attended: the great thing about Foucault's method is that you can do it yourself! Which is exactly what he proceeded to do, suggesting that there were deeply significant connections linking a relatively obscure footnote in Kant's *Critique of Judgment,* a late eighteenth-century medical training manual he had picked up, and some military proclamations he had read about in a history of the French Revolution. He then spun out a story about what these connections told us about the character of late eighteenth-century life and thought without a single reference to any other eighteenth-century texts or events. What gave him the confidence to do so was the assumption, picked up from Foucault, that in each era even the most distant texts and events share some distinctive feature.

So totality survives in postmodernist criticism as a kind of "local knowledge" about the flaws that integrate one epoch or another. But the idea of local, negative totality is just as susceptible to postmodernist criticisms as the positive form of totality that integrates all of human history. Reading any society, let alone an entire epoch, as an integrated and coherent whole, flies in the face of many of postmodernism's most valuable insights into the diversity and disconnectedness of our social practices and the language we use to describe them. And once we stop thinking about modernity as a totality, whether positive or negative, local or universal, we lose the strongest reasons for thinking that recent cultural, philosophic, and sociological innovations all work together to presage the end of modernity. That is why I describe the idea of postmodernity as an illusion generated by the fetishism of modernities.

The Self-Destruction of Modernity

I shall turn now to what is probably the most influential and suggestive part of postmodern narratives of modernity: the self-destruction of the modern or Enlightenment project. Two sorts of arguments support this claim. The first is the argument that Adorno and Horkheimer popularized in *The Dialectic of Enlightenment:* that modern humanity's conquest of nature ends up dominating and destroying the human beings that it was designed to serve. The most telling symbols of the self-defeat of Enlightenment reason in this story are environmental destruction and the Nazi death camps. This is an important, if, I believe, misleading argument. But I shall put off addressing it until the final chapter. The other sort of argument supporting claims about the self-destruction of modernity focuses on the sad fate of the revolutionary tradition that grew out of the French experience of 1789. This argument ends in the Gulag, rather than in Auschwitz. It portrays terror and totalitarianism as the unavoidable consequence of modern efforts to emancipate humanity and gain mastery of the forces that shape our political and socioeconomic lives.

The emancipation of the human subject, according to this argument, leads inevitably to the violent imposition of one particular conception of subjectivity on society.

This argument looms especially large in the stories told by many influential French radicals, like Baudrillard and Lyotard, for whom it begins as something of a self-criticism of their earlier enthusiasm for total revolution. But what begins as a form of self-criticism quickly becomes in their hands an indictment of all of modern thought, rather than just the especially abstract forms of Marxism and Maoism that inspired so many French intellectuals in the 1960s.

Like many of the more extreme versions of postmodernism, this argument rises from the bad taste that the collapse of the revolutionary tradition has left in the mouths of many French radicals. Discovering that Marxism is not true, they are inclined to declare that there is no truth.[35] Finally recognizing, after years of denying or downplaying communist terror, that intellectuals destroyed themselves in a totalitarian state by pursuing the total emancipation of humanity, they are inclined to reject all talk of emancipation as dangerous and self-destructive. In short, having discovered something deeply wrong with themselves and their revolutionary aspirations, they attribute that flaw to everyone and everything around them.

The turning of some of the last of the total revolutionaries against the intellectual tradition that nurtured them is no doubt a significant cultural event. But what does it tell us about modernity and its fate? The collapse of the revolutionary tradition represents the self-defeat of modernity only if modern self-assertion leads inevitably to the longing for total revolution. Many postmodernists seem to assume that this is the case, but I believe that they are wrong.

There is a great leap from the Enlightenment's conquest of nature to the "control and conscious mastery" of our social forces and institutions that is Marx's goal.[36] The conquest of nature demands tremendous feats of organization and the removal of constraints on rational inquiry so that we can make natural forces serve human ends. But it never demands that we be able to subject *all* social forces to our "control and conscious mastery" and thereby overcome our alienation from the world that we have created by our own efforts. It was sufficient for Enlightenment thinkers to identify and learn how to make use of the general laws that seem to govern our social and economic interactions. Alienation, the idea that we are subject to natural and social forces beyond our control, was a given for them. The task was to learn as much as possible about these forces in order to ease the human condition, not to overcome our alienation from the world.

The overcoming of alienation only becomes a major goal of radical social criticism in the wake of the failures of the French Revolution. According to the left Kantian arguments I discussed in Chapter 2, the Revolution failed because of the divisions within modern culture, the split in human character between free minds and unfree sentiments. The collapse of the ancien régime provided the opportunity for making true freedom "the principle of political association." But this "promising moment found a generation unprepared to receive it," a generation whose sentiments and character ran contrary to its noble professions of freedom.[37] You will never succeed in establishing true freedom, the left Kantians concluded, until you first create free individuals, individuals whose socialization in the world reinforced their ideas about freedom. No political freedom without the end of alienation, no genuine political emancipation without human emancipation—such are the slogans that inspired the longing for total revolution expressed in Marx's demand for the control and conscious mastery of our social powers. These slogans would not have made much sense to Locke or Hume or Montesquieu.[38]

Such demands, I believe, are indeed self-defeating.[39] And they do encourage terrible efforts to impose one's will on an ever recalcitrant world. But this revolutionary tradition represents only one stream of modern thought, no matter how influential that stream eventually became. It is a mistake to attribute its shortcomings to modern thought in general or to treat its demise as the end of the modern age.

A milder and more plausible version of the argument about the self-destruction of modernity emphasizes the widespread loss of confidence in the idea of moral and technological progress. The problem with this version of the argument is its assumption that it takes the same kind of confidence and commitment to the idea of progress and the conquest of nature to keep the juggernaut of material transformation and technological innovation going that it took to get it started in the first place. One may have needed something like Descartes' optimism about the possibility of conquering death or Bacon's confidence in the beneficent power of knowledge in order to inspire individuals to turn away from old intellectual habits and to establish cooperative societies for the investigation of nature's secrets. But once those societies have been established and once we have developed the industrial capacities to make use of their discoveries, one no longer needs such faith and commitment to keep them going. For they now produce results that people have grown used to relying upon in their everyday life. Their continued activity can be driven by much narrower and less exalted commitments than a faith in the virtues of moral and technological progress: the self-interest of the individual researcher in maintaining a well-paid and respected job, for example. That faith has been subjected to violent and repeated blows since World War I.

But the unprecedented juggernaut of material and technological change unleashed by that faith continues to run through modernity without it.

The Persistence of Modernity

Finally, let us consider the end of postmodern narratives about the decline and fall of modernity, the coming breakup into discrete and incommensurable language games that follows the end of modernity. This seems to me the least plausible part of postmodern narratives about modernity, the one that most misrepresents our current condition. We may lack today a single authoritative discourse against which to measure the value and cogency of all others. But we certainly do possess one form of discourse that transcends most local boundaries and cultural barriers. Indeed, one of the most remarkable features in our current social landscape is the ease with which one can communicate meaningfully around the world, as long as one is willing to make use of a kind of discourse associated with science, technology, and, increasingly, international capitalism. Any picture of our lives as locked up in a booming, buzzing confusion of separate but equal language games is simply inaccurate. One of these language games—with its talk of bytes and bond markets, Coca-Cola and Calvins—stands out and is reaching increasingly global proportions, while the others buzz around it more or less noisily and effectively.

The discourse associated with modern science and technology may only be a cultural "idiom" rather than the natural language against which we measure all others. It may rest on faith and consensus rather than on some indisputable act of self-grounding. And it may have no authority over large areas of our moral and political life. But whatever the strength and character of its foundations, we cannot deny its existence. One increasingly universal and powerful style of knowledge stands out from the profusion of competing language games in our world. There have been many periods in human history where knowledge and communication were deeply limited and local in character. Ours is not one of them.

This new form of knowledge, as Ernest Gellner insists,

> respects neither the culture, nor the morality, of either the society in which it was born, or of those in which it makes itself at home by diffusion. . . . One of the bitterest and most deeply felt, and alas justified, complaints against science is, precisely, that it disrupts morality. It does not, as the previous, technologically impotent learning had done, serve to underwrite social and political arrangements, and to make men feel more or less at home in the world. . . . Past belief systems were technically spurious but morally consoling. Science is the opposite. . . . Its failure to legitimate social arrangements, and to make men feel at home in the world, is the commonest charge levelled at science. The charge is entirely valid.[40]

Such, indeed, "is the world we live in, for better or for worse." To believe that we are living in some other world in which "all meaning systems are equal,"[41] requires a willful blindness to some of the most prominent features of our social landscape. We live with a style of knowledge that disrupts and displaces other styles of knowledge wherever it goes—and it seems to be going everywhere these days. A juggernaut still runs through our world. Cultural, moral, and political discourse still struggle on in the spaces to each side of the swath it cuts. The modern age continues.

The shift to postmodern culture and theory does not inaugurate a new postmodern age for a very simple reason: it lacks the power to do so. Distinctively modern ideas and practices had such power because they gave rise to science and technology. Postmodern ideas and practices, in contrast, lack such means of stopping the modern juggernaut, let alone of ushering in a new era. As a result, they may change the way in which we view and interpret our condition, but they generate nothing like the power of distinctly modern ideas to transform it.

The spectacular potency of distinctly modern ideas and practices has given rise to the illusion that new ideas necessarily lead to new epochs. It may seem that since "a change of attitude launched modernity, another change of attitude would be required to transcend it."[42] But this is to assume that another set of ideas could match modernity's extraordinary potency, which seems highly doubtful to me. Most epochs are launched by invasion, imperial collapse, or natural catastrophe, not by the diffusion of new forms of knowledge. The worldly impact of distinctly modern forms of knowledge is completely unprecedented. To expect postmodern forms of knowledge to have a similar impact on the human condition is to lose sight of one of the most important and unique features of the modern age.

Four

What's Modern
and What's Not in
Liberal Democracy?

History and Marxism are like fine wines and *haute cuisine;*
they do not really travel across the ocean.

Jean Baudrillard, *America*

Rather than ask why Americans lack a "sense of history"
we can now as well ask why Europeans have the peculiar
sense of it that they do.

Myra Jehlen, *American Incarnation*

What's modern and what's not in liberal democracy? Constitutionalism and the rule of law are not modern, even
though they develop new forms in contemporary liberal
democracies. Indeed, far from being distinctly modern, the
ideals of constitutionalism and the rule of law dispose us
to cherish historical continuity and identification with the
past. Nationalism and national loyalties, an important, if
often overlooked aspect of liberal democratic practice, are
also not distinctly modern, though they only develop in
modern times.[1] The assertion of individual rights and, with
certain qualifications, a tendency toward social equality, are
distinctly modern; an attachment to democratic forms of
government is not.

I hope that it is clear in these answers that I am talking
about the substantive rather than the temporal modernity

of things. Indeed, my reason for asking what's modern and what's not in liberal democracy is to correct the widespread conflation of the two, the tendency to assume that because liberal democracy is a new or temporally modern form of political order all of its major components must reflect the distinctively modern self-assertion of reason against tradition and received authority. By portraying modernity as a coherent and integrated whole the fetishism of modernities hides from view some of the most interesting tensions in contemporary political experience. By asking what's modern and what's not in liberal democracy, I want to draw attention to these features of liberal democratic life and to the fragile and often incongruous mix of attitudes upon which they rely.

All That Is Solid Is Not Melting

To provide an idea of the kind of incongruities that I am talking about, I begin by juxtaposing the familiar picture of modernity as a condition of ceaseless change with the extraordinarily stable horizons of everyday American political experience. The feeling of constant flux is certainly a distinctive feature of the experience of modernity. The rapidity with which technologies change, the extraordinary increase in mobility, and the acceleration of cultural change made possible by mass media all promote the sense of ceaseless motion in modern life that so repels conservatives and fascinates the intellectual avant-garde. Baudelaire, as we have seen, captured this aesthetic quality of modern life in his celebration of the ephemeral, the transient moment in the midst of eternity.[2] And Marx portrayed the much rougher social consequences of this ceaseless modern motion in his famous description of the transformative powers of capitalism.

Constant revolutionizing of production, uninterrupted disturbance of all social relations, everlasting uncertainty and
agitation, distinguish the bourgeois epoch from all earlier ones.
All fixed, fast-frozen relations, with their train of ancient and
venerable prejudices and opinions, are swept away, all new-
formed ones become antiquated before they can ossify. All that
is solid melts into air, all that is holy is profaned, and men at
last are forced to face . . . the real conditions of their lives and
their relations with their fellow men.[3]

But even Marx's bitter indictment of capitalism, it is
clear, betrays a sense of exhilaration at the extraordinary
whirl that capitalism sets in motion. Marshall Berman thus
has reason to invoke Marx in his celebration of the "experience of modernity," which he appropriately titles *All That
Is Solid Melts into the Air.*[4] Berman does a wonderful job
in this book of communicating the intense excitement, the
overstimulation of sense and intellect, that the ceaseless
motion of modern life can provide. (He also scores some
telling points against radical French postmodernists, suggesting that the disappointments that followed their one
real engagement in politics, the failed revolution of May
1968, have driven them to flee from modernity into what
he calls "a metaphysical tomb." "This postmodern world,"
Berman jokes, "makes a sensible retirement community" for
disillusioned radicals, "a great place to remain cool.")[5]

Now juxtapose this picture of modernity as ceaseless
change with a picture of liberal democratic politics in the
contemporary United States. Does this sense of transitoriness loom as large in American *political* life, where the same
two parties have completely dominated elections, even at
the local level, at least since the end of the Civil War, one
hundred and thirty years ago? Where Americans recently
celebrated the two hundredth anniversary of a constitution

that still determines, with precious few amendments, the structure of national political institutions? Where the dismissal of 15 to 20 percent of incumbents is described as an earthquake and the recent shift (in 1994) in party control of the Congress—the first in forty years—is called a revolution? I think not. Americans have an incredibly stable political horizon, as do their predecessors as exemplars of modernity, the British. This fact in itself seems sufficient for me to shatter images of modernity as an integrated and coherent whole.

Breaking with past constraints and traditional authority is one of modernity's most distinctive and celebrated activities. But it plays little role in everyday political life in America. Whatever experience of transitoriness Americans may pick up in the marketplace,[6] the workplace, or in their cultural lives develops alongside firm and, for the most part, unquestioned expectations of political stability. Despite their well-documented contempt for the men and women that they choose to fill political offices, Americans seem to have little doubt that these offices, and the structure of government that they define, will survive into the foreseeable future. The stability of political expectations in many modern societies often goes unnoticed, given the noisy and ever-changing conflicts that occupy the foreground of the political scene in large liberal democracies. But it is just as significant—and, indeed, almost as novel—as the experience of transitoriness in the life of the citizens of distinctly modern societies. For the *political* equivalent of the experience that everything solid is melting into air, we would have to turn to very different societies, such as Russia during its Civil War, or Weimar Germany during the great inflation of 1923, or the peculiar netherworld between communism and capitalism that many East Europeans now occupy.

For a more positive vision of a fully modernist political life, we need to turn to political theory. The most sustained attempt, at least to my knowledge, to paint a picture of political life that mirrors modernity's attachment to ceaseless change and tradition-smashing, is Roberto Unger's massive three-volume work, *Politics*.[7] Unger, the most philosophic and best educated of the group of radical law professors who call themselves Critical Legal Theorists, published this enormously ambitious work in 1988. It was not very successful in fulfilling its primary purpose: to provide a positive program for the critical legal theorists, a group that has been repeatedly criticized for their relentless negativity about contemporary institutions. But in trying to match the critical legal theorists' penchant for "trashing" legal and political authority with an alternative model of political order,[8] Unger produced an extraordinarily thorough vision of a society in which modernist sentiments would shape political as well as cultural life. Looking at that vision for a moment will help bring into relief the tremendous distance between liberal democratic politics and the ceaseless tradition-breaking of modernist culture.

> Suppose . . . a society whose formative system of powers and rights is continuously on the line, a system neither invisible nor protected against ordinary conflict; a society in which the collective experience of setting the terms of social life passes increasingly into the tenor of everyday experience.[9]

This is Unger's vision of an emancipated society. Such a society needs institutions that would open themselves up to constant challenge and revision, that could never generate fixed and immovable forms of hierarchy and domination. These institutions "must invite conflict rather than suppress it." They support a constitution that possesses, according to Unger, "a remarkable property. It is designed to prevent any definite institutional order from taking hold in social life; there lies its structure-destroying effect."[10] The most important and idiosyncratic of these practices is something that Unger calls "destabilization rights," rights that "protect the citizen's interest in breaking open the large-scale organizations or the extended areas of social practice that remain closed to the destabilizing effects of ordinary conflict and thereby sustain insulated hierarchies of power and advantage."[11] Destabilization rights entitle citizens to challenge every social institution that threatens to remove structures of domination from conflict and revision. Under antitrust legislation, government lawyers are supposed to bring suit to break up monopoly control over particular economic goods. In Unger's emancipated society *all* citizens would have the right to challenge and break up *all* practices that support the monopolization of power by individuals or groups. Everyday life in Unger's "superliberal" society would be an endless round of challenge and counterchallenge in the "zone of heightened mutual vulnerability" created by the realization that no sphere of activity is immune to conflict. No wonder Unger insists that the inhabitants of his society "must be haughty, high-spirited, and even reckless."[12]

Until now, Unger notes, such a life of proud and reckless autonomy was available only to a small minority of individuals: the aristocratic master of slaves or serfs, the prophet of new religions, or the avant-garde artist. But in Unger's emancipated society that life will be available to all. For that society will be like "a religion in which all people are both priests and prophets," and in which ordinary citizens become "more like the [avant-garde] poet, whose visionary heightening of expressed emotion may border on unintelligibility and aphasia."[13] Even if it were possible to create such a society—and it is certainly *not* possible—most of us, I suspect, would find its obsessive contentiousness extremely unpleasant and distasteful.[14]

Nevertheless, there is much in Unger's vision of an emancipated society that resonates with distinctly modern ideas and aspirations. If, like Unger, you believe that "true satisfaction can be found only in an activity that enables people to fight back, individually or collectively, against the established settings of their lives,"[15] then you too might dream of his structure-denying political structures. Unger has imagined a political society that would fully satisfy distinctly modern longings to assert one's reason and freedom against received authority. In doing so, he makes it very clear just how little everyday life in liberal democracies embodies modern gestures of self-assertion against settled traditions and authorities.

This notion that liberal democratic politics should somehow embody the modern self-assertion of reason and freedom also inspires much more sober and level-headed visions than Unger's. Consider, for example, Jürgen Habermas's vision of what he calls the "unfinished project of modernity."[16]

Habermas develops this vision as a counterweight to postmodernist critiques of modern rationalism. As I noted in the previous chapter, one influential strand of postmodernism suggests that modernity is now complete and has shown its true, terrifying face in the death camps built by Hitler and Stalin. In this grand postmodern metanarrative, the self-assertion of subjective reason ends with the imposition of totalitarian order by willful subjects. Habermas counters this view of modernity by arguing that the "project of modernity" is not the imposition of a single, diversity-stifling rational order, but rather the "enrichment of everyday life" that unfolds when "objective science, universal morality and law, and autonomous art" develop in their separate spheres "according to their own inner logic."[17]

This project, according to Habermas, remains unfinished primarily because of our failure to bring morality and politics into line with the free and rational standards that he has long argued are grounded in uncoerced communication and consensus.

Habermas understands very well that modern science "does not, as the previous, technologically impotent learning had done, serve to underwrite social and political arrangements, and to make men feel more or less at home in the world."[18] But he believes that the modern self-assertion of reason generates appropriate standards for art and morality that parallel and fit together coherently with those that govern scientific research. To complete the project of modernity, we would have to bring our moral and political standards into line with those generated by uncoerced communication and consensus.

I do not want to get bogged down here in the controversies about Habermas's theory of communicative competence. I am interested, instead, in the way in which he constructs a vision of modernity as a diverse but still coherent and integrated whole. Habermas, it should be said, is heir to both traditions of discourse that I have identified (in Chapter 2) as sources of the fetishism of modernities. He inherited the left Kantian critique of modernity as a negative totality from Adorno and the Frankfurt school. And he inherited the picture of modernity as a process of rationalization and disenchantment from Weber and German social theory. His insistence that the separate but equal standards of science, morality, and art complement each other and all fit together into a coherent "project of modernity" reflects, I believe, the lingering influence of the fetishism of modernities.[19]

Treating modernity as an integrated and coherent whole helps Habermas overlook the dependence of some of the political practices he favors on attitudes that are inconsistent with rational self-assertion and uncoerced communication. Take, for example, his recent defense of what he calls "constitutional patriotism."[20] Habermas invents this concept in a very worthy cause: combatting the surge of ethnic chauvinism that has risen in the wake of German reunification. As an alternative to inherited racial, cultural, and ethnic ties, he proposes loyalty to the liberal democratic principles of the postwar German constitution as a focus for German identity. Such constitutional patriotism, he hopes, will satisfy the need for group loyalty without encouraging dangerous and irrational beliefs in inherited German identity and communal destiny. One can only hope that he is right.

But constitutional patriotism, when effective, is more than simple loyalty to a particular set of principles. The longer it lasts, the more it becomes loyalty to *our* principles, the principles we have lived by and our ancestors have lived by, not just loyalty to rationally valid principles. In other words, constitutional patriotism also generates settled identities that act as inherited political constraints. One need only look to the United States, the most obvious and successful example of constitutional patriotism, to confirm this claim. It would be very helpful for the future of liberal democracy if Germans were to replace visions of blood and soil with American constitution worship. But in doing so, they would be trading one form of inherited identity for another, not replacing inherited identities with principled loyalties generated by uncoerced communication.[21]

The notion that there is a single modern "project" that establishes parallel standards for science, art, and morality is an illusion fostered by the fetishism of modernities.[22] Pursuing that illusion usually leads either to dreams of total revolution or to the various versions of the utopia of unlimited contestation that Unger and Lyotard, among others, celebrate. Habermas's sobriety and genuine appreciation for the virtues of contemporary liberal democracies prevents him from endorsing either of these two options. But the pursuit of this illusion leads to his strained and misleading characterization of familiar liberal democratic practices.

I see two major sources of this illusion that modern self-assertion sustains a single modern project to reorder the standards of science, art, and morality. The first is the fierceness of the Enlightenment's critique of inherited hierarchy and religious authority, a critique expressed most ferociously by Diderot's hope to see the day that the last king is strangled with the guts of the last priest. I cite Diderot's famous declaration to make the point that for all the talk of "the heavenly city of the 18th century philosophers,"[23] the most deeply felt political goals of the philosophes were primarily negative in character: to end the arbitrary and irrational power of people who only took the trouble to be born to noble parents and to eliminate the Church's stifling demands for moral and intellectual conformity. The philosophes were considerably less strongly committed to any particular replacements for these ancien régime institutions.

The other source of this illusion that liberal democracy is an integral part of a single project of rational self-assertion has to do with the peculiar circumstances and impact of the French Revolution. The ease and speed with which feudalism, the French monarchy, and the Catholic hierarchy collapsed in 1789 made a tremendous impression on those who lived through it. The witnesses to the Revolution experienced something that was quite unimaginable before it happened: the possibility of simply discarding the weight of the past and subjecting human institutions to rational direction and control.

The concept of right now made itself felt all at once, and the old framework of injustice could offer no resistance to it. . . . Only now does man come to recognize that thought ought to govern spiritual reality. Thus it was a splendid dawn. All thinking beings shared in the celebration of this epoch.[24]

This extraordinary experience, this heady sense that the givenness of things no longer posed an obstacle to the improvement of the human condition, has haunted Western political culture ever since 1789.[25] For it greatly expanded our imagination of political possibility. Later generations have dreamt of recovering the revolutionary moment when the dead weight of the past seemed to have been lifted from the people's backs. Utopia, the older vision of a rationally controlled society, was always imagined as existing beyond the realm of historical time and political action. The Revolution, in contrast, took place within history and the real-world conditions for action. Yet it seemed to promise the possibility of a "mythic present" free from all past constraints.[26] Once recorded and commented upon by the revolutionary generation, this experience of increased possibility has stuck in the imagination of modern political theorists and actors, whether as an object of longing or of dread.

When remembered in this way, the Revolution seems to represent "the master narrative of modernity,"[27] the natural political complement to the self-assertion of reason in modern science. The Revolution, from this point of view, "invented democratic culture" and "most of our ideas and practices of politics."[28] And liberal democracy's achievements and failures appear, from this perspective, as an integral part of modern reason's rebellion against tradition and received authority.

The problem with this point of view is that, not to put too fine a point on it, the Revolution was a political failure.

The Revolution certainly gave Europe a powerful kick in a democratic direction by undermining aristocratic privileges. But many of the institutions that secured a future for liberal democracy, parliamentary representation and constitutionalism, for example, developed earlier and elsewhere and did not really develop strong roots in France until well after World War II. (This is why it is not so strange that François Furet thought that the late 1970s was finally the right time to declare that "the Revolution is over" for the French.)[29] Moreover, they did not develop as part of a self-assertive rebellion against tradition and received authority. English parliamentarianism was not established without blood and rebellion; but it maintained and cherished its historical roots. American constitutionalism may have been established to prove that human beings are not "forever destined to depend for their political constitutions on accident and force." But it also counted upon the "veneration which time bestows on everything" old to support its innovations.[30]

The Revolution gave birth to a project that was never on the agenda of Enlightenment thought: to institutionalize the exhilarating moment of liberation from the dead weight of the past by realizing autonomy in our practices and institutions.[31] The young Hegel, Marx, the critical theorists, Roberto Unger, and even Habermas, in his peculiar way, all participate in this project. But we should not confuse this revolutionary project with the liberal democratic ideals and institutions that so many intellectuals associate with modern political culture. The revolutionary project is an attempt to complete the modern self-assertion of reason with a set of truly rational and uncoercive institutions. Liberal democracy, in contrast, has a much more ambiguous relationship to tradition and the self-assertion of reason, as I shall try to demonstrate in the following brief tour of its most important ideals and institutions.

Constitutionalism

I have already suggested that the practice of constitutionalism runs counter to the modern assertion of reason against tradition and received authority by disposing us to value precedent and historical continuity. There is a sense, however, in which constitution-making, American-style, follows from an attachment to the self-assertion of reason. For written constitutions are often attempts to establish and enforce what are seen as rational principles of government. But the creation of some body of fundamental law, especially when it is written down in a constitution, establishes a founding moment that in a successful regime quickly becomes a traditional object of reverence—something that Madison, for one, understood very well indeed and was ready to exploit in defense of the American Constitution. He rejected Jefferson's proposal to have frequent and regular constitutional conventions because it would deprive the Constitution of the "veneration which time bestows on everything, and without which even the wisest and freest governments would not possess the requisite stability." "In a nation of philosophers," he adds, "this consideration ought to be disregarded." But "in every other nation, the most rational government will not find it a superfluous advantage to have the prejudices of the community on its side."[32]

For the founders of constitutions, the horizon of the past may look like an unbroken record of tyranny and irrationality. But that is not how things appear to the citizens of the regimes they establish. For them, there is at least one bright, shining deed that stands out on the horizon of the past and guides them in the present: the constitution. As a result, the past contains for them inspirational as well as cautionary tales, tales that are especially cherishable because they are their *own* as well as instructive. The great manufacturers of our disposable consumer goods may teach us that "history is bunk"; the practice of constitutional democracy teaches otherwise. Of course, constitutional piety often serves as a mask for complacency, innovation, or simple self-interest. But the very need for this kind of legitimation points to the positive feelings toward the past and our political ancestors that constitutionalism keeps alive in liberal democracies.

In the United States this kind of ancestor worship begins with the Constitution and spreads to most political practice. Think of how difficult it is to change even the most absurd and irrational American political traditions, such as the reliance on the New Hampshire primary as a means of determining who is fit to win the Republican or Democratic nomination for president. Americans may not learn much about history. But what they learn about their political history they tend to revere.

It is high time, in any case, to junk the old image of the United States as a land without history, as an eternal youth among nations.[33] This image is as old as the American republic.[34] As Oscar Wilde once joked, the eternal youth of Americans, it seems, "is their oldest tradition."[35] But the image of America's eternal youth persists today, even in the latest and most fashionable European commentaries. Jean Baudrillard, for example, proclaims in his postmodernist sendup of American culture that "history and Marxism are like fine wines and *haute cuisine;* they do not really travel across the ocean."[36] However plausible this image may once have been, it makes little sense today. After more than two hundred years under the same constitution, Americans have a sense of political continuity with the past that can be found almost nowhere else in the contemporary world.[37] Even the greatest interruption of American political history, the Civil War, now seems to most Americans to be a chapter in that continuing story, rather than a break with a distant past.[38] Most European and Asian nations, in contrast, have great and unassimilated discontinuities in their recent political histories. Their longer cultural horizons may make Americans seem rootless in comparison to them. But a longer and more continuous political horizon provides Americans with a much more settled sense of legal and political identity.

The Rule of Law

Even the attachment of liberal democracies to the rule of law, which is a considerably less tradition-bound notion than constitutionalism, promotes a positive attitude toward the past and historical continuity. As a political ideal, the rule of law encourages us to exercise power and resolve our differences primarily by means of general rules and principles that apply to all members of a community.[39] Whatever reason we may choose to support this ideal, in practice it promotes a prejudice in favor of historical continuity. For, as Aristotle pointed out long ago, "the law has no power to compel obedience beside the force of habit, and habit only grows up in the long lapse of time, so that lightly to change from the existing laws to other new laws is to weaken the power of the law."[40] To be governed by laws, rather than men, as the rule-of-law rhetoric demands, we have to be familiar with a body of general rules and principles to guide us. Frequent changes in laws, even if it means replacing imperfect laws with better ones, make it exceedingly difficult to be guided by law rather than the will of political leaders. As a result, the rule of law promotes dispositions in favor of historical continuity and against the tradition-challenging attitudes associated with the modern self-assertion of reason.

This favorable disposition toward precedent and legal continuity deeply disturbed some of the most radical Enlightenment reformers. Jeremy Bentham, to take the most extreme example, devoted a considerable amount of time to ridiculing this disposition and the irrationality it inspires. In his *Handbook of Political Fallacies* he heaped contempt on all the arguments, such as "the wisdom of our ancestors," "one step at a time," "good in theory, bad in practice," that we invoke to limit legal and political innovation, arguments that remain prominent to this day, despite his savage and hilarious caricatures of them. If, Bentham writes, a plan to reform some familiar institution

> departs in ever so slight a degree of routine, the practical man, the man of routine, does not know what to make of it. . . . What he has been used to is always to consider whether the new plan is similar, in matter and form, to his previous practices. If it happens to be different, it throws him into a sort of perplexity. If the plan is a good one, and good reasons have been advanced in its favor, so that he feels unable to contest them or to bring forward preponderant disadvantages, he will be afraid of committing himself by pronouncing it bad. In order to show his candor, especially if he is on good terms with you, he may go so far as to admit that the plan is good, that is in *theory* . . . but, alas, bad in practice.[41]

Doesn't that sound familiar? Isn't this the first response of the average undergraduate to every alternative vision of political life that one presents in courses on the history of political thought? Couldn't one pick out parallel statements from contemporary American debates about every serious reform proposal, from health care to social security?

Bentham's utilitarian radicalism has had a great impact on many aspects of liberal democratic life. But it has barely made a dent in the prejudice in favor of historical continuity promoted by constitutionalism and the rule of law.

Individual Rights

The assertion of individual rights in liberal democratic politics, unlike constitutionalism and the rule of law, fits in quite well with the modern self-assertion of reason and subjective freedom. It fits in particularly well with the Enlightenment project of generating, collecting, and disseminating useful knowledge, as J. S. Mill makes clear in his famous utilitarian justification of freedom of speech and association in Chapter 2 of *On Liberty*. Without freedom of speech and association, there could be no republic of letters to gather, sort, and spread the fruits of knowledge yielded by the modern self-assertion of reason.

There is nothing controversial about this association of individual rights and modernity, so I will not elaborate on it here. I do, however, want to say something about the relationship between liberal constitutionalism and the assertion of individual rights. One is tempted to say that liberal constitutionalism, with its focus on individual rights, is the distinctly modern form of constitutionalism. In a temporal sense, this is undoubtedly true. Although constitutionalism is a very old practice, constitutionalism as a means of establishing and guaranteeing the exercise of a set of basic individual rights is relatively new. But with regard to the substantive sense of modernity, the assertion of reason against received authority, liberal constitutionalism is torn between its distinctly modern end, the assertion of individual rights, and its distinctly nonmodern means, the power of the past over the present established in the authority of the Constitution. The assertion of individual rights looks forward; it seeks to secure departures from the familiar and authoritative. Constitutionalism protects such departures by encouraging us to look back into the past for authoritative guidance. As a result, even the least text-bound versions of liberal constitutionalism, such as Ronald Dworkin's vision of constitutional rights, have a backward-looking component.[42]

Liberal constitutionalism, it has often been noted, involves the paradox of self-limitation. It asks us to bind ourselves, like Ulysses before the sirens, in order to protect ourselves in the future from our freedom-destroying inclinations.[43] By doing so, liberal constitutionalism also promotes conflicting character dispositions. On the one hand, it fosters a culture of rights, a culture of individual self-assertion against the dead weight of history. On the other hand, the means it uses to secure these rights promote a certain degree of reverence toward legal and political traditions. That is why Roberto Unger insisted that in a truly emancipated society, constitutional practices would have to be self-subverting, not just self-limiting. But a self-subverting constitution, unlike self-limiting institutions, is an illusion.[44] Constitutional rules cannot empower us to act freely in some areas unless they constrain us in others. When these constraints are associated with a founding document and a body of fundamental law, they are bound to counter our disposition to assert independence from the demands of tradition and continuity.

Social Equality and Democracy

I would also argue that, with important qualifications, a commitment to a certain kind of social equality is distinctly modern. The assertion of reason against received authority brings traditional and inherited legal hierarchies into doubt. And it supports the belief that, at least outside of the family, no one individual should have legal authority over another simply because of the accidents of birth. This is the Enlightenment's great contribution to the French Revolution. Nowhere was the Revolution more representative of distinctly modern ideas than in its attack on feudal privileges.

This tendency toward social equality is confirmed and reinforced by the world of high technology and industrial production that modern self-assertion helps bring into being. The constantly changing techniques and patterns of association promoted by this form of production undercut the settled sense of time and place that support aristocratic hierarchies. As a result, industrial society produces individuals trained to cut loose from inherited ways of doing things. It gives birth to the creature that Ernest Gellner calls the "modular man": an individual with a certain basic level of education who can be plugged into different specialized settings as productive techniques change, rather than the bearer of the specialized skills that master craftsmen pass on to their children and apprentices.[45] This common educational core gives the modular men of industrial society a kind of equality that conflicts with aristocratic beliefs about inherited social hierarchies.[46]

This identification of social equality with modernity, however, has to be qualified in at least two important ways. First of all, while distinctly modern ideas and practices promote equality of legal status, they do not necessarily promote equal conditions of existence. They undermine the inherited legal and social hierarchies of aristocratic society but not necessarily inequalities of wealth. We are thus concerned here with the kind of equality Tocqueville described in *Democracy in America*: the end of inherited legal and social privilege, rather than the end of inherited wealth.

Second, it is important to note that the modern self-assertion of reason is not a wholehearted ally of legal equality. It also gives rise to scientific theories about racial, class, and gender hierarchies that have often taken the place of traditional understandings of the inequalities of birth. Such theories reflect an assertion of human reason to discover the objective hierarchies in the nature of things, as opposed to the hierarchies that follow from the stories that we tell about the deeds and origins of our ancestors. There is thus nothing antimodern about nineteenth- and twentieth-century theories about racial superiority and inferiority, even if we have good reason for thinking them wrong. They often employ the latest scientific techniques and theories and satisfy genuine intellectual curiosity. Traditional prejudices may frequently find a place in them, encouraging their authors to jump to unwarranted conclusions that serve the interests of already dominant races; but these theories still draw facts and inspiration from the modern self-assertion of reason. Accordingly, it makes sense to describe them as distinctly modern, rather than as the return of the repressed and unenlightened sentiments of our "tribal" past. The social equality that modernity promotes with one hand, it is fully capable of taking away with the other.

Democracy's ties to distinctly modern ideas and practices are even more tenuous. One can argue about whether democracy is distinctly modern in the temporal sense. Your answer will depend on how much weight you place on inclusiveness in your definition of democracy; for inclusiveness is the quality in which contemporary liberal democracies outshine their ancient Greek predecessors. But it is hard to characterize democracy as a substantively modern practice, except in the negative sense that majority rule remains one of the only available principles to legitimate political power after the inherited hierarchies of aristocratic society fall into disrepute. The positive ideals of democracy, popular participation, the rule of public opinion, and the glorification of the common man all run up hard against modern commitments to rationalism, efficiency, and the distrust of mere opinion. It is easy to argue that technocracy and meritocracy fit much better with the rational self-assertion that grounds science and industrial society than majority rule, even though these principles do not provide sufficient public legitimation of political power in most modern societies.

Perhaps that helps explain the peculiar position of democracy in our lives. On the one hand, democratic principles have a certain cultural hegemony in contemporary liberal democracies. Politicians cannot explicitly argue against these principles. And even hostility to modern commitments to social and political equality usually has to disguise itself as a defense of some deeper or more traditional understanding of democracy in order to get a hearing. (For example, consider Allan Bloom's best-seller, *The Closing of the American Mind*. It is subtitled *How Higher Education Has Failed Democracy and Impoverished the Souls of Today's Students*, even though one of the most important ways in which Bloom thinks education has "impoverished the souls" of our students is by its assertive egalitarianism.) On the other hand, the cultural hegemony of democratic principles seems to have little impact on the management of political, legal, and especially socioeconomic institutions, all of which seem to emphasize the possession of special skills and expertise, rather than popular participation.

Conclusion

The purpose of this brief tour through the ideals and institutions of contemporary liberal democracies was to provide a glimpse of some of the tensions and complexities that emerge when we stop looking at our political world through the lens of the fetishism of modernities. If the liberal democratic regime is, as the American Constitution has been described, "a machine that would go of itself,"[47] then it resembles a Rube Goldberg contraption much more than a sleek modern factory. It may draw much of its strength from the forward-looking power of the modern self-assertion of reason. But it also contains numerous devices that work against and redirect distinctly modern attitudes. It is a clumsier and more fragile machine than it appears to be when viewed as part of the coherent and integrated whole of modernity. But it is also a more flexible and adaptable machine, since it has such a large and diverse assemblage of working parts.

Five

Disentangling
Theory and Practice
in the Modern World

> What characterizes and defines our intellectual situation
> is precisely the wealth of contents that can no longer be
> mastered. . . . We will perish from this, or overcome it by
> becoming a spiritually stronger type of human being. But
> then it makes no sense from a human point of view to try
> to wish away this enormous danger and hope by stealing
> from the facts, through a false skepticism, the weight of
> their facticity.
>
> Robert Musil, "Mind and Experience: Notes for Readers
> Who've Escaped the Decline of the West"

We intellectuals, I think it is fair to say, tend to exaggerate
the importance of our discoveries. Like the cartographers
whom Montaigne ridicules in his essay on cannibals,[1] we
often behave as if we were entitled to redraw the map of
the world just because we have seen Jerusalem or whatever
other corner of the universe our efforts have uncovered.

The fetishism of modernities feeds and feeds on this intellectual vice. If we think of modernity as a coherent and
integrated whole, then every discovery that we make, no
matter how narrow or specialized, potentially has a crucial
bearing on the fate of the world. Such hopes have sustained
generations of scholars through years of thankless drudgery
in the archives. Think of Marxists struggling to identify the

precise conditions for capital accumulation in some obscure corner of Europe. The research may seem esoteric, but if capital was accumulated in an unexpected way in Estonia, then that might alter our understanding of the logic of capitalist development; and if we alter our understanding of the logic of capitalist development, we may have to alter our understanding of the basic constraints of modern life and our hopes for transcending them.

The days in which scholars struggled to make sense of obscure corners of the socioeconomic world in the hope of hastening the Marxist millennium are probably over. These days, we seem much more likely to overestimate the power of theory to shape practice than the reverse. Heideggerian claims that metaphysics "grounds" the modern age and "holds complete dominion over all the phenomena that distinguish" it tend to be taken much more seriously today than Marxist materialism.[2] Ironically, theory has never seemed more powerful, more capable of shaping reality in its own image, than it is today, when it seems less capable than ever of justifying itself and its insights. There is nothing, it seems, that theoretical discourse cannot make us do today—except, perhaps, endorse its claims to have discovered the truth.

In this chapter I look at the exaggeration of theory's power to shape reality that, I believe, sustains some of the most familiar and influential critiques of modernity, such as Heidegger's arguments about technology and Adorno and Horkheimer's story about the "dialectic of enlightenment." I do not, however, want to underestimate that power. For, as I argued at the end of Chapter 3 on the idea of postmodernity, the spectacular and unprecedented potency of modern theories, in particular their ability to transform the way we do things through science and technology, is probably the most unique feature of the modern age. The challenge, then, is to find ways of speaking about the distinctive power of modern theory without falling into the exaggerations encouraged by the tendency to treat modernity as a coherent and integrated whole.

Before I begin, however, let me say briefly what I mean by the terms theory and practice. By theory I mean simply the accounts that we give of the world and our place in it. By practice, I mean the way we do things. It is important for what follows to emphasize that there are theoretical as well as social practices, i.e., there are distinctive ways of giving accounts of ourselves and the world. The ways in which theory is practised can and, as we shall see, do come into conflict with the claims that theories advance. For example, there was never a more dedicated or obsessive truth-seeker in the history of philosophy than Nietzsche, the great philosophic enemy of truth-seeking. He sacrificed his health, his happiness, perhaps even his sanity to making sense of the burdens under which he believed modern individuals suffered. Not all critics of truth-seeking, however, display this conflict between their theories and the way in which they theorize. Foucault, I believe, resembles Nietzsche in this regard, his repeated critiques of truth-seeking notwithstanding; Derrida, I suspect, does not. That makes Foucault and Nietzsche less consistent than Derrida, but considerably more interesting.

Modernity as a "Project"

The most striking evidence of the current exaggeration of theory's power to transform practice is the increasingly commonplace description of modernity as a "project," a description that we have come across repeatedly in previous chapters. When Leo Strauss described modernity as a philosophic project during the 1950s and 1960s he was usually dismissed as an eccentric idealist. But by the time (1987) his student Allan Bloom described modernity in this way in his best-seller *The Closing of the American Mind,*[3] this view was right in the mainstream of social criticism. By then the expression "the project of modernity" had become a commonplace in the ongoing debates about the meaning and fate of modernity.[4]

What does it mean to speak of modernity as a project? This expression has become so familiar that its oddness is no longer striking. Certainly, we describe no other historical period in this way. No one would think to describe classical antiquity, let alone the Christian Middle Ages as a philosophic project, no matter how much he or she might admire Plato, Aristotle, or Augustine. We do not even seem comfortable describing the Renaissance as a project, although, as with modernity, we identify the Renaissance with the emergence of a set of distinctive intellectual aspirations, namely, the recovery of ancient art and knowledge.

The description of modernity as a project gains its plausibility from two of its most distinctive features as a historical category. The first of these is the fact that the modern age, unlike other epochs, existed first as a shared idea or aspiration and only later as a shared condition. The founders of modern science and philosophy, unlike the intellectual heroes of the Renaissance, thought of themselves as trying to start afresh, thereby freeing humanity from the weight of past prejudices and illusions. As a result, "modernity was the first and only age that understood itself as an epoch";[5] and it did so right from the start. That would probably be enough to justify speaking of a *modern* project, that is, a shared effort to bring into the world certain distinctly modern ways of doing things. But to justify speaking of *modernity* itself as a project assumes that this endeavor is responsible in some way for establishing the basic conditions of social existence in the modern age. What makes this assumption plausible is the unprecedented power to transform the conditions of everyday life that modern theory gains from its connection to the new sciences and technologies. Theorists in other ages may have dreamt of launching new eras with their innovations, as some postmodernists do now, but they never had anything like this power to turn their dreams into epochmaking transformations.

But just how much and what part of modernity is a projection of the modern self-assertion of reason onto reality? I have argued throughout this work that there is good reason to associate the modern juggernaut of technological change and demystification with the innovations of early modern theorists. But something more than that is implied in the way in which modernity is often characterized as a project.

Listen to the way in which Marcuse uses the expression. "Advanced industrial society," he argues, "is the realization of a specific project." "As that project unfolds, it shapes the entire universe of discourse and action; . . . it circumscribes an entire culture; it projects a historical totality, a world."[6] Modernity, according to this view, is the historical totality within which characteristically modern ideas and practices develop, a way of being that gradually "swallows up or repulses all alternatives."[7] As such, it is a framework within which things happen, rather than a blueprint for action. It is a narrow and constraining pattern that has been projected onto the structure of our lives, like a pattern of light and shadow projected onto the backdrop of a stage.

To make sense of this way of talking about modernity as a kind of projection, we have to go back to its intellectual roots in phenomenology and Heidegger's critique of modern science and philosophy. An obsession with projects and even with the idea of projects is, as we shall see, characteristic of early modern thought. But talk about modernity or the Enlightenment itself as a project does not, as far as I can tell, emerge until the 1930s and 1940s. This way of talking about modernity combines two meanings of the term project: as a shared design or enterprise and as a projected background or framework within which we think and act.

The first and more familiar of these meanings appears prominently in early modern scientific and philosophic writings. Bacon, the thinker with whom the idea of the modern project is most closely associated,[8] speaks, for example, of his desire to leave "some outline and project of that which he had conceived" as evidence "of his honest mind and inclination towards the benefit of the human race."[9] A plea to Louis XIV to support the establishment of the Académie des Sciences argued that "its project is so great, and it will be so glorious to the state, and so useful to the public, it is not possible that your majesty, who has projects so vast and magnificent, would not approve and favor it."[10] Moreover, the program of scientific research as a means of gathering useful knowledge that Bacon and his supporters promoted set off a veritable mania for projects for improvement of the human condition.[11] Some of these projects were fanciful and harebrained, as Swift makes hilariously clear in his parody of the scientists of the Royal Academy in the Laputa section of *Gulliver's Travels.*[12] He ridicules the "projectors" of his fictional academy as mindless enthusiasts for research who are blind to the absurd or harmful character of the ends that they pursue. He is helped in writing his satire by the fact that "projector" was a common term for a swindler or speculator at the time as well as for a promoter of designs for improvement[13] (an ambiguity that contemporary critics of the modern project would, no doubt, love to be in a position to exploit).

This sense of a project as a design for improvement through scientific research is clearly present in characterizations of modernity as a project. But these characterizations treat the project of modernity as a shared social condition as well as a shared design. How should we link these two meanings? The simplest way would be to treat modernity itself as the result of the project undertaken by Bacon and his early modern followers. Their project with all of its flaws and virtues, one could then say, has been projected into our existence. That is, in effect, how Leo Strauss and his followers talk about the project of modernity. The flaws of modernity, for him, are the flaws of modern philosophy—and not because he treats modernity itself as a set of philosophic ideas and attitudes, but because he believes that a specific set of consciously chosen philosophic ideas and attitudes have produced the modern social condition.[14] But since relatively few contemporary philosophers and social critics are willing to accept so boldly idealist a vision of history, this view cannot explain the origins of the characterization of modernity as a project. To do so, I suggest, we have to go back to phenomenology and Heideggerian critiques of modern thought—whence, in any case, I suspect Strauss derived the idea himself.

"Project" and "projection" are key terms in phenomenology, terms that point to the way in which understanding always involves the projection of meaning and purpose into the world of things.[15] The philosophic use of these terms was expanded and popularized primarily by Sartre and Heidegger. Sartre turned the idea of the project into the central moment of an existentialist philosophy of action and commitment. Acting, Sartre argues, always involves an ultimately groundless commitment to the world of possibilities projected by our choice to do one thing rather than another. He spoke, in particular, of the "fundamental project" that each of us must choose and the resolution we must make to live in the world of possibilities created by our choice.[16] I suspect that it was the widespread attention given to Sartre and existentialism that is most responsible for the return of the term project to a position of prominence in philosophic discourse. Today, it seems, it is a lazy philosopher or social critic indeed who has no "project" to pursue.

Heidegger also starts with the phenomenological concept of projection. But he builds on it a critique of modern scientific and philosophic thought rather than a vision of heroic action. It is this critique, I believe, that is the most important source of the contemporary characterization of modernity as a project.

Projection is a key category already in Heidegger's *Being and Time*. Understanding, Heidegger argues there, always involves the projection of a world of possibilities within which things gain their meaning. This kind of project, he emphasizes, "has nothing to do" with the subjective planning we ordinarily associate with the term. On the contrary, Heidegger argues that we ourselves are projects, thrown into a limited range of possibilities by the particular ways of projecting a world in which we discover ourselves.[17]

Heidegger draws heavily on this understanding of projection in the critical analysis of modern science and philosophy that he began in the 1930s. "Every sort of thought," he argues in *What Is a Thing?* "is always only the execution and consequence of the historical mode of being [*Dasein*] at that time, of the fundamental position taken toward what is and toward the way in which what is, is manifest as such." Modern science and philosophy are made possible, according to Heidegger, by the projection of a new mode of being, a new world of possibilities within which things can gain their meaning. This "*project* establishes a uniformity of all bodies according to relations of space, time, and motion." Its "mode of questioning" and cognition of nature are "no longer ruled by traditional opinions and concepts." For natural bodies no longer have "concealed qualities, powers and capacities." They "are now only what they show themselves as, within this projected realm"; and within this realm, they can "show themselves only in the relations of places and time points and in the measures of mass and working forces."[18]

Heidegger's point here is that modern science and philosophy emerge as possibilities only within the world projected by this new mode of understanding. As such, they represent moves within the limited range of alternatives established by this project, rather than direct confrontations with the structure of physical realities. This is a profound and important insight that, I believe, has enriched our understanding of the origins and limitations of modern thought. Notice, however, that there is nothing in this way of talking about the modern project that identifies it with the shared and conscious efforts of Enlightenment thinkers to transform the world. The project of modernity, for Heidegger, is the mode of understanding *within* which characteristically modern ideas and practices emerge, rather than a collective plan to rebuild the world in the image of modern philosophy.

If, however, you combine these two different ways of talking about projects, as a shared enterprise and as a background framework, you arrive at the vision of the modern project that occurs most frequently in contemporary debates: the basic patterns of modern life, patterns that have been established by the efforts of Enlightenment philosophers to promote human emancipation and a rational society. This way of talking about the modern project was spread by students of Heidegger's thought, such as Kojève, Strauss, and Marcuse, and by numerous other German philosophers and social critics, such as Adorno, Horkheimer, and Habermas. Today, as I noted, it has become such a commonplace that its Heideggerian roots are very difficult to see.

Subjectivizing Heidegger's understanding of the modern project in this way makes it a much more satisfying focus for narratives about modernity's rise and fall. For it gives modernity a set of philosophic heroes and villains that makes its story far more touching and dramatic. Moreover, it opens up heroic roles for contemporary theorists to play as the proponents of a new, postmodern project. But regardless of whether one views modernity as something projected by philosophers or projected on us by fate or being, this way of characterizing modernity tremendously exaggerates the power of theory to shape practice in its image.

This exaggeration becomes especially clear when one takes a sober look at Heidegger's tremendously influential critique of modern technology. For Heidegger, we are living within the constrictive framework of the modern projection of a world of uniformly moving and calculable bodies. In such a world, our needs and interests become the only acceptable measures of reality, which is why Heidegger insists that the modern period "is defined by the fact that man becomes the measure and center of all things."[19] External reality, in this world, becomes a mere "standing-reserve" of objects to be employed for our benefit or edification, a reserve that we are exhausting at an alarming rate as we seek the "absolute dominion over the entire earth that prods modern man."[20] Great rivers like the Rhine may still flow through our landscapes. But for us, Heidegger argues, they exist "in no other way than" as a "power supplier" or "an object on call for inspection by a tour group ordered there by the vacation industry."[21] Even Kant's "starry heavens" above us,[22] it seems, are losing their capacity to inspire awe since they began to be filled with satellites beaming back useful information to us. "I was frightened," Heidegger confesses to his interviewer from *Der Spiegel* "when I saw pictures coming from the moon to earth."[23] Even the limitless heavens, the last refuge of contemplative philosophers,[24] seems to be falling under the sway of human purpose and calculation. All that "we have left," Heidegger complains, are "purely technological relations."[25]

As I noted in the Introduction, the undeniable power of this nightmare vision of modernity depends on the way in which it makes us feel that the modern project is filling out the whole horizon of modern life and thought. "Monstrousness" reigns in Heidegger's exploited river Rhine only to the extent that we believe that we will soon be able to view things *"in no other way"* than as objects on call to our needs. Heidegger is hardly so foolish as to believe that we are reaching the point of gaining complete control over the forces of nature. But he does believe that the instrumental understanding of the world embedded in the modern project is crowding out all other ways of relating to being. It is in this sense that he believes that modern metaphysics "holds complete dominion over *all* the phenomena that distinguish the [modern] age" (emphasis added).[26]

How plausible is this view? Let us return for a moment to the starry sky and those pictures being sent to us from the moon. For Heidegger, this is a frightening image because it suggests that the modern vision of a world of calculable and useful objects is being projected even onto the seemingly infinite depths of the night sky. For me it suggests, to the contrary, the relative weakness of human endeavors. All of that extraordinary concentration of resources and intelligence just to send human beings a distance, that from a cosmic perspective, is hardly around the block! Projecting human purposiveness into the vastness of space tends, for me, to cut it down to size, by dispelling our illusions about the extent of our ability to master reality.

Is the glass half-empty or half-full? Do our efforts to travel and communicate beyond the earth magnify or deflate our pride? I suppose it depends on how you look at it. But my point is that we *can* and *do* look at it in both ways. Heidegger is right to think that the projection of a world of calculable quantities is one of the background conditions for the success of modern science and that it is a powerful framework within which much of what is most distinctive about modern life and thought unfold. He is wrong, however, to think that it crowds out all other frameworks and ways of picturing reality.

I have often thought that Heidegger's vision of modernity reflects the forest dweller's, as opposed to the coast dweller's, perspective on the relation between being and human purpose. If, like Heidegger, we derive our connection to being from the profound depth and stillness of an old-growth forest, then technology is certainly capable of uprooting us and crowding out any other way of viewing the world, for it is capable of completely destroying such a forest, let alone its depth and stillness. On the coast, in contrast, we can always turn our backs on human civilization, even in the midst of the tackiest of Floridian or Californian resorts, and touch base with something larger than ourselves by gazing out to the sea and the endless horizon. The coexistence of contemplative and instrumental attitudes toward nature seems much more plausible there than in the middle of the Black Forest, where the two attitudes inevitably come into a much starker conflict.

The contemplative attitude toward natural existence is alive and well in the modern world, especially in the natural sciences. Its importance in the more speculative sciences is obvious from the way in which cosmologists and theoretical physicists talk about their work. But it seems alive and well even in the more earthbound sciences, such as chemistry, as was brought home to me by a recent episode of the PBS science series *Nova*. It was a documentary about the discovery of Carbon 60, a new kind of complex molecule that took an extraordinary and completely unexpected form similar to that of Buckminster Fuller's geodesic domes. Accordingly, these molecules were dubbed "Buckyballs" by their discoverers, who eventually received a Nobel prize for their efforts. The kind of delight and amazement these chemists expressed at the form of these molecules has much more to do with the "wonder" that, according to Aristotle, grounds contemplative philosophy than with the projection of human purpose and calculation into nature.[27]

The contemplative attitude toward nature may have lost quite a bit of the prestige and authority it once had, since it cannot deliver the goods that its rival can produce in so much abundance. But I see no reason to equate its loss of prestige and authority with its gradual disappearance. Selfless wonder at the marvels of existence frequently thrives in the modern world, as with many scientists, right alongside a much more purely instrumental or reductive attitude toward nature. As a result, we often see a mix of competing dispositions in scientific research, with considerable tension between the content of many theories and the way in which these theories are practiced. But this mix is no more or less incoherent than the mix of dispositions toward tradition and continuity that, as I argued in the previous chapter, sustain many liberal democratic practices and institutions. The tendency to think of modernity as a coherent and integrated whole blinds thinkers like Heidegger to this inconsistent mix of dispositions toward existence and leads them to exaggerate the power of distinctly modern ideas to crowd out other ways of imagining oneself in the world.

Indeed, I would go so far as to suggest that the kind of theories that Heidegger is challenging are particularly ill-suited to the totalizing role that he assigns to them. The strength of these theories lies primarily in their predictive power, the power that gives them an unprecedented ability to alter and improve the way we do things. Their corresponding weakness lies in the uncertainty they create "about what 'totality' this continuing success" at altering reality "could ever bring forth."[28]

Modern science and philosophy decidedly do not "serve to underwrite social and political arrangements, and to make us feel more or less at home and at ease with the world" in the way that earlier, less technologically powerful theories had done.[29] As a result, they rarely provide us with the sense of an all-encompassing order of things that could crowd out all other ways of looking at the world. This seems to be part of the price we pay—or is it a fringe benefit?—for our greater ability to control our environment and transform the way we do things. Older theories compensated for their technological impotence with a far greater ability to shape the imagination. Distinctly modern theories compensate us for their disruption of a coherent vision of the world with the material goods they produce, the pains they prevent, and the room for choice among conflicting alternatives they open up.

The Dialectic of Enlightenment

Or so they *seem* to compensate us, until we begin to suspect that we are the victims rather than the beneficiaries of the new forces that they have put into the world. This suspicion brings me to Adorno and Horkheimer's argument about the dialectic of enlightenment, the second of the two arguments about modern theory's impact on practice that I want to look at in this chapter.

The basic outlines of this argument have become quite familiar, almost commonplace, in contemporary discourse about modernity. According to this argument, the Enlightenment is a self-defeating project. Enlightenment thinkers strove to liberate us from arbitrary and irrational traditions so that they could learn how to make nature best serve our needs. But by learning how to dominate nature, we have also learned how to dominate ourselves far more effectively than we had ever done in the past. As a result, our "unprecedented domination of nature ends in our unprecedented subordination to our own creations."[30]

As I noted in Chapter 3, this argument plays a central role in the counternarratives that some postmodernists construct about the rise and fall of modernity. If the modern project of human emancipation defeats itself in this way, if it ends up as the promoter of new technologies of mind control and mass murder, one might well conclude that the modern age is over. Who would willingly continue along such a path to self-destruction?

In evaluating this argument about the dialectic of enlightenment, we face another situation in which one wonders whether the glass is half-full or half-empty. On the one hand, there can be little doubt that scientific and technological innovations have unleashed upon us previously unimagined powers of destruction. These innovations, at the very least, are necessary conditions for most of the great manmade disasters of the twentieth century, such as World War I, the death camps, and environmental devastation. On the other hand, they are also the source of an extraordinary and growing list of accomplishments that extend and enhance human life. It is very hard indeed for someone who has just been returned to an active life by a successful quadruple bypass operation to think of himself as a victim of his own creations. Modern history does not stop at Auschwitz. Some paths in modernity lead there, or to Hiroshima or to Chernobyl. Most do not.

How should we judge the balance between these two impressions of modernity? We certainly cannot afford to assume that we have all learned our lesson about the dangers of boundless technological progress. It may be hard to believe that a naive faith in the radiant and unblemished future promised by science and reason could survive the manmade disasters of the twentieth century. But persist it does in many places, not the least of which is the office of that Republican revolutionary, Newt Gingrich. Moreover, the success of Francis Fukuyama's recent book[31] makes it clear that many intellectuals still get a charge out of playing with the idea of a triumphant end of history in which our only serious problem is boredom.

So we have good reason to keep a spotlight shining on the destructive potential of technology; to encourage people to treat scientific claims with some of the same skepticism that they are used to employing when evaluating religious and traditional authorities; and to keep reminding academics and politicians that scientific descriptions of society often create the facts that they claim to uncover. But such actions bring us to a more cautious and self-critical appreciation of modern achievements, rather than to the end of modernity. For they rest on the belief that highly destructive events are merely possible rather than necessary effects of modern innovations, and that greater self-awareness can significantly diminish their frequency and impact.

Dialectic of enlightenment arguments, in contrast, tend to treat catastrophe as a necessary, rather than a merely possible, outcome of the modern project. Although they focus on the failure of the Enlightenment to achieve its goals, they still ascribe tremendous power to its ideas. For they argue as if the inner contradictions of Enlightenment thought completely dominate modern existence, so that some sign of our subordination to the forces that we have created lies at the end of every modern road.

The justification of these claims, however, is quite tenuous. It is easy to show, for example, that modern innovations in weapons, transport, and organization were necessary preconditions for the Holocaust. But so were numerous other factors that have nothing to do with distinctly modern ideas and practices. It is easy to show that Nazi sympathies represented something more than the return of the repressed and barbaric passions of a premodern past. But it is considerably harder to take seriously the idea that Weimar Germany was suffering from anything like "an excess of rationalism."[32]

To a certain extent, Adorno and Horkheimer rely on mere association with something so horrible and irrational as Nazism to establish the strength of their critique of Enlightenment rationalism. As such, their argument takes the form that Leo Strauss once described as the *reductio ad Hitlerum,* an argument that allows one to dismiss out of hand anything that is even remotely associated with Hitler's success.[33]

But dialectic of enlightenment arguments, I believe, derive most of their persuasiveness from a mode of argument that Albert Hirschman calls "the perversity thesis." The structure of this mode of argument, Hirschman explains, "is admirably simple, whereas the claim being made is rather extreme." Here are some examples. "Attempts to reach for liberty will make society sink into slavery, the quest for more democracy will produce oligarchy and tyranny, and social welfare programs will create more, rather than less, poverty."

It is not just asserted that a movement or a policy will fall short of its goal or will occasion unexpected costs or negative side effects: rather, so goes the argument, the attempt to push society in a certain direction will result in its moving, all right, but in the opposite direction. Simple, intriguing, and devastating (if true), the argument has proven popular with generations of "reactionaries" as well as with the public at large.[34]

What stronger condemnation of a new policy or practice could there be than the suggestion that it enhances the very evils it is designed to eliminate? Who would want to have anything to do with such senseless innovations?

Hirschman describes this mode of argument as part of an attempt to map out what he calls "the rhetoric of reaction." Clearly, conservative and reactionary rhetoric has a special affinity for perverse effects arguments, since these arguments promote a distrust of innovation and activism. If it looks like "everything backfires," why should we even attempt to improve things? But I think that it should also be clear that radical as well as reactionary and conservative social critics are drawn to arguments about perverse effects. Indeed, the most influential of all perverse effects arguments is probably Marx's critique of capitalism. The more our productive capacities grow under capitalism, Marx argues, the worse off an ever-increasing majority of people becomes. This perverse effect is unavoidable, he insists, as long as we stick to a capitalist mode of production, since capitalism's unprecedented expansion of our productive forces is fueled by the increasing exploitation of labor. Dialectic of enlightenment arguments focus on different causes and consequences, but take a similar form: our unprecedented emancipation from natural constraints and traditional authorities lead to an ever more onerous and complete subordination to the powers that we have created to serve us.

The rhetorical power of perverse effects arguments clouds our judgment in at least two important ways. First of all, it lowers the standards of evidence that we would ordinarily demand as proof that a new policy or practice is responsible for certain bad consequences. The idea that some innovation is promoting the very evil that it seeks to eliminate is so damning and, I must add, intriguing that it grabs our imagination even before we have seen good evidence that this is what has really happened. And it tends to keep that grip on our imagination even as convincing counterevidence against it begins to pile up. As a result, perverse effects arguments are often advanced quite casually, as if they do not require much evidence, like the claim that Allan Bloom tosses out in *The Closing of the American Mind* that affirmative action is leading to the resegregation of society. Such claims are often taken quite seriously, even though they frequently make little effort to deal with mountains of counterevidence and are often supported by nothing more than a telling anecdote or a casual observation, such as Bloom's discovery that African-American students tended to eat together in University of Chicago dining halls.[35] Marx, I would suggest, developed his theory of capitalism's perverse effects long before he had anything like convincing evidence to back it up and clung to it even after he began to see the evidence that workers' wages were not falling in Western Europe.[36] Clearly, one of the things that drew him to this theory was the immensely satisfying prospect of being able to explain with a single cause both the extraordinary growth of production and the suffering of workers in the modern world.

Perverse effects rhetoric also creates guilt by association. The discovery that some practice serves the very cause it opposes is so devastating that it quickly taints our appreciation for similar or related practices, even if we have little evidence that they too lead to perverse effects. This kind of guilt by association accounts, for example, for much of the current strength of conservative arguments against the welfare state. It is arguable, but not at all implausible, that programs like AFDC (welfare payments for unemployed parents of dependent children) perpetuate rather than eliminate poverty. But the possibility that this particular welfare program may produce perverse effects taints almost all other welfare programs in conservative rhetoric, even when there is little or no evidence that they too have produced perverse consequences. Similarly, the perverse effects that follow from Soviet-style central planning of economies has tainted the image of all forms of government intervention in the economy, as if, say, progressive taxation or national health insurance also necessarily produce perverse effects.

Dialectic of enlightenment arguments benefit from both of these tendencies of perverse effects rhetoric. The claim that the Enlightenment defeats itself, that the striving for human emancipation creates even more powerful forms of domination, is so striking, such a dramatic climax to a story about modernity, that it tends to grab our imagination and crowd out less exciting but more plausible claims.[37] And even the possibility of such perverse effects in some areas of modern science, such as weapons technology, tends to create a kind of guilt by association that is projected onto the entire epoch of modernity, a process that gives modernity the appearance of forming an integrated and self-defeating whole. Dialectic of enlightenment arguments provide useful correctives to naive and uncritical faith in the emancipatory power of science and technology. But they exaggerate the power of theory to determine the course of events, as if the whole of modern experience necessarily unfolds out of the internal logic and inconsistencies of Enlightenment thought.

Treating modernity as a coherent and integrated whole tends to fetishize modern thought and experience, turning modernity into a demonic and single-minded power that frustrates our hopes and haunts our dreams. This fetishization of modernity is especially clear in Heidegger's work. In Heidegger's vision, the spirit of modernity hovers over our lives like some Gnostic demiurge, contaminating every aspect of modern theory and practice and leaving us only with the hope that if we wait quietly and attentively enough we might hear the distant otherworldly call of the savior God, Being.

The fetishism of modernities once tended to broaden and deepen rebellious and revolutionary sentiments. For if the spirit of modern society is perceived as pervading all aspects of our life, then reform and even partial revolution will seem ineffective. Only a *total* revolution in our whole mode of life and feeling could be successful in removing such an obstacle to happiness.[38] Today, with the collapse of hopes for such a revolution, the fetishism of modernities is much more likely to promote an exaggerated passivity than the longing for total revolution. For if the spirit of modernity does indeed inform every aspect of our life and thought, then it will also inform and defeat our efforts to change things. Heidegger's passive attentiveness or Adorno's retreat to aesthetic experience may seem like the only rational options in such a situation.

But these extremely pessimistic visions of the modern predicament rest on the assumption that all of the forces in modern life line up in the same direction, an assumption that I hope to have brought into serious doubt in this book. We do not have to claim either contra-causal freedom or a knowledge of history's emancipatory line of march in order to challenge these pessimistic visions of our predicament. All we need to do is show that many of the cultural, political, and scientific forces in our lives move in competing and often inconsistent directions. When we realize that we are not dangling "from the puppet strings of some hobgoblin of fate, but on the contrary, that we are draped with a multitude of small haphazardly linked weights," then we regain considerable room for maneuver.[39] The very fact that we are being pushed and pulled in different directions makes it possible to deal critically with the influence of any particular idea or practice. We may not be able to throw off either the weight of the past or of distinctly modern achievements, but we do have much more of an opportunity to shift burdens and alter the balance of forces in our lives than would appear from any picture of modernity as a coherent and integrated whole.

Social critics like Heidegger and Adorno have made extremely important contributions to our efforts to deal with these forces: for example, by drawing attention to the unstated premises of scientific thinking and by exposing its tendency to impose order on the social world while claiming to discover it. But such contributions are not sufficient for them. Like Montaigne's cartographers,[40] once they have discovered their Jerusalem they proceed to redraw the map of the entire world so that all the lines of force and influence move in the same direction as the new forms of domination that they have identified.

Facing the Facts

I had originally titled this chapter "Disconnecting Theory and Practice in the Modern World." I dropped that title for a very simple reason. The commonsense belief that theory and practice influence each other seems unimpeachable to me, so it would be very foolish indeed to talk about "disconnecting theory and practice." Theories do not arise in a vacuum, whatever their authors may say about them. And practices cannot escape the influence of theories, if only because we need concepts to recognize and engage in them.

What I had in mind when I came up with the original title was a concern about how easily we tend to move from commonsense beliefs about the mutual influence of theory and practice to the much more questionable position that theory and practice embody each other. Alisdair MacIntyre, for example, starts in *After Virtue* with the commonsense position. "Every action," he notes, "is the bearer and expression of more or less theory-laden beliefs and concepts; every piece of theorizing and every expression of belief is a political and moral action."[41] But he then uses this reasonable assumption to justify his claim that "the transition into modernity was a transition both in theory and in practice and a single transition at that." Great political figures from the Medici to Napoleon, MacIntyre argues, must be

> understood as expressing in their actions . . . the very same conceptual changes which at the level of philosophical theory are articulated by Machiavelli and Hobbes, by Diderot and Condorcet, by Hume and Adam Smith and Kant. . . . [For] abstract changes in moral concepts are always embodied in real, particular events.[42]

Similarly, Michael Sandel begins with the uncontroversial assumption that "to engage in a political practice is already to stand in relation to theory." But he treats this assumption as if it justifies his rather idealist "view about politics and philosophy and the relation between them—that our practices and institutions are themselves embodiments of theory"[43] (a view that leads him to discover all of the flaws of John Rawls's theory of justice embodied in contemporary liberal practices and institutions).

Abstract theories, no doubt, have *some* effect on *some* particular events. And events, no doubt, have *some* effect on *some* theories. But why assume that theories "are *always embodied*" in events and practices unless one assumes beforehand that a society forms a coherent and integrated whole? The mutual influence of theory and practice is one thing, their mutual embodiment quite another.

Tangling theory and practice together in this way has become popular for a number of reasons. It allows us, as we have seen, to lean on leading theories as a guide to the interpretation of our practices, even when we doubt the validity of these theories. (Consider the way in which communitarians like Sandel and MacIntyre first condemn liberal theory's portrait of "unencumbered" selves as a distortion of our social natures and then complain about the way in which contemporary liberal practices and institutions turn us into precisely the kind of dissociated individuals we thought they had dismissed as a mere figment of the liberal theorist's imagination.)[44] It also lends plausibility to our claims to have discovered our favorite moral or political principles conveniently embedded in our practices. (Think of how Rawls is able to respond to those who complained about his overly Kantian and asocial view of the self in *A Theory of Justice* by quickly discovering Kantian principles of moral personality "embedded" in our democratic public culture.)[45] And, of course, it has become popular because of the way in which it magnifies the significance of our discoveries, as I mentioned at the beginning of this chapter.

Tangling up theory and practice in this way also helps us deal with or, more accurately, evade the consequences of one of modernity's most characteristic features: the explosion and ever-increasing differentiation of knowledge. The loss of mastery over knowledge, our increasing inability to integrate this ever-swelling flood of insights and information into settled and coherent patterns, is a problem that every modern intellectual has to deal with, sooner or later. Enlightenment efforts to generate, preserve, and disseminate useful knowledge have been successful beyond the philosophes' wildest dreams. It is often disorienting and disheartening—even if it is frequently exhilarating as well—to live with the ever-swelling flood of new knowledge created by the universities, research networks, and government institutions that these efforts helped bring into being. For this flood sweeps away familiar assumptions and reassuring guideposts with alarming regularity. And it reduces at an ever-accelerating rate the relative significance of the knowledge that a single individual can master.

Treating modernity as a coherent and integrated whole, a whole in which theory and practice embody each other, represents one way of reasserting control over this flow of knowledge. One may not be able to comprehend, let alone assimilate, the vast range of insights and theories produced by today's knowledge mills. But if one can portray them as an outgrowth of a single historically specific and limited worldview—for example, as the fruit of an indefensible metaphysical projection (Heidegger) or of a self-defeating drive for domination (Adorno)—then one can master this knowledge by closing it off within a partial and questionable horizon. True, each day the sciences may be producing great quantities of new and discomforting knowledge about human beings and their place in the universe. But armed with portraits of modernity as a coherent and integrated whole, humanists can reassert mastery over this knowledge by noting how it is constrained by modern assumptions and paradigms that the humanists alone can fully comprehend.

Robert Musil provides an incisive criticism of these attempts to regain control over the growth of new knowledge in the modern world when he suggests that:

> What characterizes and defines our intellectual situation is precisely the wealth of contents that can no longer be mastered. . . . We will perish from this, or overcome it by becoming a spiritually stronger type of human being. But then it makes no sense from a human point of view to try to wish away this enormous danger and hope by stealing from the facts, through a false skepticism, the weight of their facticity.[46]

Closing the horizon of modern theory and practice wishes away the challenge posed by modernity's profusion of new and disorienting knowledge with a reassuring but ultimately false skepticism about our knowledge of the world. It may be reassuring to be able to bracket the disturbing and unwieldy profusion of facts as reflections of a distinctly modern and questionable worldview. But that will not make those facts go away or help us face the challenges that they pose to us. And it is a *false* skepticism that provides such reassurance since it is a skepticism rooted in a claim to know the truth about modernity, the reality behind its congratulatory self-image, rather than in doubts about the possibility of knowledge.[47]

The historicist skepticism promoted by Heidegger, Adorno, and many postmodern critics of modernity dismisses the possibility of gaining access to the truth about the natural world. But it seems quite comfortable with assertions about the truth or essence of historical developments, at least with regard to modernity and its consequences. This skepticism is as much a reassertion of the primacy of historical and textual knowledge as it is a challenge to our claims to understand the way things are. It does not so much deny the facticity of the discoveries of modern science as it brackets and subordinates them to the claims of a more historical and textual form of knowledge. A drive to master nature and all of its creatures may well inspire much of modern science and philosophy, as critics of modernity like Heidegger and Adorno repeatedly complain. But a drive to reassert mastery over human knowledge, I believe it is fair to say, inspires much of their critique of modern science and the world it has helped bring into being.

Conclusion

Of all the views put forward in the current debate about modernity, I am probably most sympathetic to the ideas about "reflexive modernization" advanced by Anthony Giddens and Ulrich Beck, among others.[1] Giddens and Beck argue that we are entering a period in which the skeptical, self-testing rationality ordinarily associated with distinctly modern ideas and practices is now being turned on those ideas and practices themselves. The impact of this chastened, self-critical attitude toward modernity appears most clearly in the increased popularity of environmental constraints on industrial development. It also appears in the increasing reluctance to seek economic and technological solutions to moral and social problems.

But even this chastened attitude towards distinctly modern ideas and practices is susceptible to the fetishism of modernities, as can be seen from the rhetoric with which Beck launches the idea of reflexive modernization. Rather than merely highlight the emergence of a more cautious and self-critical approach to modernity, Beck declares that we are entering "the transition from one social epoch to another." "Reflexive modernization," he suggests, "opens paths to an alternative modernity." It "means the possibility of a creative (self)destruction for an entire epoch: that of industrial society."[2] Accordingly, Beck looks for signs of this chastened, self-critical form of modernity everywhere in our lives, even in the most unlikely corners of the modern world. For instance, in this new "alternative modernity," he argues, the modern focus on technological expertise drops away. In "risk society" (Beck's term for his alternative modernity) "no one is an expert, or everyone is an expert."[3]

Why is it that contemporary intellectuals cannot uncover a new or hidden development without declaring the coming of a new epoch in human experience? Every sensible observer would probably acknowledge the growing importance of some of the reflexive ideas and practices that Beck describes. But why the need to jump to conclusions about an epochmaking transformation in the character of human association? Why the need to exaggerate the impact of these new developments, as in Beck's claims about the delegitimation of technical expertise in contemporary society?[4]

Everyone, it seems, still wants to ride the wave of history. Never mind the fact that the very idea that history flows in a single direction is a manifestation of precisely the kind of unchastened, unreflective modern thinking that so many contemporary intellectuals explicitly reject. As we have seen,[5] even postmodernists like Lyotard, people who ordinarily disdain unilinear history and grand historical narratives, seem to want to ride the wave of history onto a new postmodern shore. The legitimation and empowerment to be gained for one's ideas by claiming to hold the key to the new age seems just too attractive to resist, even if doing so relies on precisely the kind of thinking about reason and progress that the new era is supposed to leave behind.

In addition, contemporary intellectuals, it seems to me, often suffer from a kind of "modernity envy" when characterizing the new developments they have uncovered. They often talk as if these developments do not deserve our attention unless their impact is as deep or as pervasive as that attributed to distinctly modern ideas and practices. Unless these developments promise the kind of epochmaking transformation associated with distinctly modern ideas and practices, there seems, in any case, little room for them in our lives, given the way in which modernity has been portrayed as a coherent and integrated whole.

You do not, however, have to deny the existence of distinctly modern ideas and practices or the importance of their impact on our lives—certainly, I do not—in order to get over this kind of modernity envy. There are many things in human history that will never be the same again as the result of the influence of distinctly modern ways of thinking and acting. But that does *not* mean that everything from now on will *share* a distinctly modern quality—at least until a new postmodern quality takes its place. Nor does it mean that from now on all we will have to choose from are variants of a *single*, distinctly modern model of society—at least until that model and its variants will be supplanted by another singular model of association. It only means that distinctly modern ideas and practices are bound to be part of the different mixtures of ways of thinking and acting that are emerging in different parts of our world.

We are not experiencing today anything like "the end of modernity" or the transformation of one form of modernity into another. We are experiencing, instead, the collapse of a particular illusion about modernity: the illusion that there are specific forms of cultural and political life that express or complete the distinctive achievements of modern science, technology, and industrial production. It should be clear now, with the globalization of distinctly modern ideas and practices, that the achievements of modern science and industry are compatible with a variety of cultures and forms of political organization. The uniquely rapid and successful industrialization of East Asian nations, if nothing else, forces us to acknowledge the possibility of previously unsuspected combinations and mixtures of cultural, political, and socioeconomic practices. Recent social, intellectual, and cultural changes do not spell the end of modernity for the simple reason that modernity never existed as the kind of integrated and coherent whole whose death is now being proclaimed. Modernity, in this form at least, is a "never was" rather than a "has been."

The decline of modernism in aesthetics should spell the end of the illusion that the autonomy and alienation of the avant-garde artist is the appropriate and inevitable complement to the dynamism of advanced industrial societies. There was a time when the prominence of modernist styles in art and especially architecture suggested a deep coherence between aesthetic culture and the rapid pace of the modern juggernaut. But that time has passed, a fascinating moment in modern history rather than an abiding condition of modern life. Similarly, the collapse of the European revolutionary tradition should spell the end of the illusion that there is some specific form of political organization that can bring to a conclusion the process of emancipation from tradition and contingency inspired by distinctly modern ideas and practices. The belief that the French Revolution started a process of building the distinctly modern form of political culture, a process that it would just take one more revolution to complete, gave rise to this illusion. But that belief has evaporated as it has become ever more difficult to figure out where such a process might be taking us.

For many intellectuals, the end of these illusions about modernity is bound to be rather unsettling and deflating: unsettling because it creates tremendous uncertainty about the future, deflating because it undermines the privileged position that so many of them have claimed as prophets of history's line of march. But it is a false comfort that allows us to reinterpret the great surprises of modern history— such as the rise of nationalism in supposedly individualist, commercial societies, the triumph of Nazi brutality in one of

Europe's most modern and civilized nations, or the extraordinary success of capitalism in East Asia—in a way that neatly fits them into already familiar models of modern and postmodern society. And it is a dangerous and self-deluding privilege that intellectuals usurp when they claim knowledge of the direction towards which history is marching.

For myself, I find the prospect of the end of these illusions both frightening and exhilarating. It is frightening because recent history makes it all too clear that many of the coming surprises are bound to be unpleasant. It is exhilarating, however, because it opens our eyes to combinations and mixtures of ideas and practices that are far more interesting to explore than the overly uniform models offered by modernist and postmodernist thinkers. The fear I take to be salutary. If we are going to walk through an uncharted minefield then it is foolish to delude ourselves into thinking that we know where all the mines are laid. The exhilaration I find valuable as well. For it sustains the kind of curiosity about the world, the expectation of learning something important that we do not already know, that should accompany all inquiries into the way things are. The world, past, present, and future, offers far stranger and more unexpected combinations of things than are dreamt of in modernist and postmodernist philosophies. It is time to get on with the task of studying and dealing with them.

Notes

Introduction. The Fetishism of Modernities and the Secret Thereof

1. André Gide, quoted in A. Hamilton, *The Appeal of Fascism,* xxi–xxii. Gide's Nietzschean justification for this position is that "man does nothing great without constraint, and those capable of finding this constraint within themselves are very rare." He offers this argument to justify his siding with the Bolsheviks. (He wrote these words a few years before his eye-opening tour of the Soviet Union in 1936.) But he recognizes that, according to this argument, "if I approve of Soviet constraint I must also approve of Fascist discipline."

2. This is so even though many of its advocates frequently insist that they are not talking about modernity as an epoch at all. I discuss the self-contradictions of the invocation of the end of modernity by many postmodernists in Chapter 3.

3. A. Borgmann, *Crossing the Postmodern Divide.*

4. J. Habermas, "Modernity vs. Postmodernity." See also U. Beck, *Risk Society: Towards a New Modernity;* U. Beck, A. Giddens, and S. Lash, *Reflexive Modernization;* A. Feenberg, *Alternative Modernity;* S. Toulmin, *Cosmopolis: The Hidden Agenda of Modernity;* and A. Touraine, *Critique of Modernity.*

5. G. Vattimo, *The Transparent Society,* 2.

6. D. Kolb, *The Critique of Pure Modernity,* 261.

7. See A. Giddens, *Consequences of Modernity,* 47, for a similar complaint about postmodernist rhetoric. Fredric Jameson (*Postmodernism,* xi–xii) describes this self-contradiction as postmodernism's "constitutive impurity." It might seem at first glance that this tension in postmodern thinking represents little more

than the recurring difficulty faced by all defenders of relativist or historicist theories of truth: that one cannot refute nonrelativist theories without claiming for relativism a kind of universal validity that relativism itself declares illegitimate. But I do not think that this is the case. One could easily undermine modernity's grand historical narratives of progress and emancipation without replacing them with an alternative "postmodern" narrative. One need only point out the ways in which many modern intellectuals deluded themselves into thinking that history moves in a single and coherent direction. That would allow us to develop a much deeper and more plausible picture of what has been called modernity by concentrating on the great variety of recent practices and experiences that do not fit the models of traditional, modern, or for that matter, postmodern society. In effect, that is what Steven Seidman challenges postmodern social theorists to do in "The End of Sociological Theory," 128–29.

8. As the French anthropologist of science, Bruno Latour, concludes in *We Never Have Been Modern.*

9. J. F. Lyotard, *The Postmodern Condition,* 82; G. Vattimo, *The Transparent Society,* 8.

10. K. Marx, *Capital,* 81–96.

11. H. Schnädelbach, "Die Aktualität der 'Dialektik der Aufklärung,'" 241. See also P. Wehling, *Moderne als Sozialmythos,* 10, 15.

12. Ibid., 241.

13. H. Marcuse, *One-Dimensional Man,* xvi. "When technics become a universal form of material production, it circumscribes an entire culture; it projects a historical totality, a world" (ibid., 154).

14. In *The Longing for Total Revolution,* 18–27, 98–125, I examine the important role in radical social criticism of the idea of the spirit of modern society as the ultimate obstacle to the satisfaction of our aims and desires.

15. See the first half of Chapter 2 below.

16. See Richard Wolin, *The Politics of Being,* 143–45, and R. Pippin, *Modernism as a Philosophical Problem,* 138–39.

17. Totality, of course, was not always such a disreputable concept. Only thirteen years ago (1984) Martin Jay could publish a well-received history of the concept of totality (*Marxism and Totality*) that treated each step in the direction of the concept as an "advance." For an account of the persistence of the idea of totality among some of its most vehement critics, such as Adorno and Foucault, see J. Grumley, *History and Totality: Radical Historicism from Hegel to Foucault*.

18. M. Heidegger, *Nietzsche*, vol. 3, 174–75.

19. M. Heidegger, "The Age of the World Picture," 115.

20. M. Heidegger, "The Question Concerning Technology," 16.

21. Ibid., 17ff.

22. I discuss Heidegger's critique of modernity more fully in Chapter 5.

23. For notable exceptions, see D. Kolb, *The Critique of Pure Modernity*, 259–65, and H. Schnädelbach, "Die Aktualität der 'Dialektik der Aufklärung'" and "Gescheiterte Moderne?" in Schnädelbach, *Zur Rehabilitierung des Animal Rationale*, 241, 432–34. See also P. Osborne, *The Politics of Time*, and N. Rengger, *Political Theory, Modernity, and Postmodernity*. When commentators, such as Alain Touraine, call for a "critical investigation of the idea of modernity" (*Critique of Modernity*, 4), what they usually have in mind is a reconsideration of what makes modernity what it is, in other words, an investigation of different conceptions of modernity rather than an examination of the concept of modernity itself.

24. D. Kolb, *The Critique of Pure Modernity*, 263.

25. H. Blumenberg, *The Legitimacy of the Modern Age*, 467.

26. R. Musil, "Helpless Europe," *Precision and Soul*, 119–20. See the epigraph at the head of this introduction for the passage cited here.

27. A. Megill, *Prophets of Extremity*, 346.

28. This is an example of what Ernest Gellner (in *Legitimacy of Belief*, 46–55) calls a "reendorsement" theory: if a particular characterization of ourselves and the world is no longer plausible in the light of developing standards of critical reason, simply reendorse it as an edifying myth or story.

29. Among the most insightful of these studies are David Kolb's *The Critique of Pure Modernity* and Robert Pippin's *Modernism as a Philosophic Problem.*

One. Imagining the Modern Age

1. W. Connolly, *Political Theory and Modernity,* 1–3.
2. See H. R. Jauss, "Literärische Tradition und gegenwärtiges Bewusstsein der Modernität"; M. Callinescu, *Five Faces of Modernity,* 13; J. Le Goff, *History and Memory.*
3. See H. R. Jauss, "Literärische Tradition und gegenwärtiges Bewusstsein der Modernität," 11. J. Le Goff, *History and Memory,* 40–43.
4. Indeed, this usage of modernity is not listed in the 1989 edition of the *Oxford English Dictionary.*
5. The German title of Habermas's book is *Die philosophische Diskurs der Moderne.* For the development of the German terms associated with the idea of modernity, see H.-U. Gumbrecht, "Modern, Modernität, Moderne." On the development of the term *Neuzeit,* see R. Koselleck, *"Neuzeit:* Remarks on the Modern Conception of Movement."
6. Ironically, one of the most powerful arguments that modern philosophers from Bacon to Bentham have advanced for breaking with the past and traditional authority is that *we,* the most recent generation, *not* our ancestors, have the experience and greater wisdom of old age. The antiquity of our ancestors, they argue, is an illusion of perspective. From our point of view, looking back at times past, they appear old. But from the perspective of historical development, they are mere youths. It is we, Bacon declares, who have the right to claim the title of wisdom that goes along with age and experience, not the so-called "ancients." See F. Bacon, *The New Organon,* #84, pp. 501–2, and *The Advancement of Learning,* 189. For the career of this trope, see R. Jones, *Ancients and Moderns,* and R. Merton, *On the Shoulders of Giants.* For a later echo of this argument, see J. Bentham, *Handbook of Political Fallacies,* 43–45.

7. W. Connolly, *Political Theory and Modernity*, 3.

8. T. Adorno, *Minima Moralia*, 9. See also M. Foucault, "What Is Enlightenment?" 39.

9. We could then, for example, be free to talk about the "postmodern" qualities of ironic and self-subverting literary works such as *Don Quixote* or *Tristram Shandy* without feeling anachronistic. (Of course, one might also begin to wonder whether "postmodern" is the best term to characterize these qualities of irony, self-reference, and disjointed narrative, if these qualities can play so prominent a role in classic works written in the sixteenth and eighteenth centuries.)

10. J. Le Goff, *History and Memory*, 23.

11. One might argue that these new forms of fundamentalism would never have arisen without the provocation provided by distinctively modern forms of secularism. In that case, modernity would be a necessary condition for the emergence of these sects. But it still would make little sense to describe them as modern in the substantive sense.

12. See R. Pippin, *Modernism as a Philosophical Problem*, 16–19.

13. David Kolb (*The Critique of Pure Modernity*, 263) similarly distinguishes this plausible conception of the modern age from the implausible conception of modernity as an integrated whole. "If we want," he argues, "we can still name our age "modern" in honor of dominant features of our multiple inhabitation, but modernity is not the single unifying meaning of our world."

14. One reason that there is so much debate and uncertainty about the "origins" of modernity is that it is a substantive, not a temporal, conception of modernity that is at stake in most contemporary discussions of modernity. The origins of modernity therefore lie in the emergence of new ideas and practices, not in the dividing line created by some historical discontinuity. The period of time that most of us conventionally describe as the modern age did not begin with a decisive event or catastrophe— such as a new divine revelation or a devastating war or the col-

lapse of a world empire—that impressed itself on observers as a sharp dividing line between present and past experience. It began, instead, with a set of distinctive ideas, the so-called modern project associated with Bacon, Descartes, and the Encyclopedists. But when we talk about the origins of modernity, it is hard to keep the temporal sense of the term from informing our judgments. As a result, we look for temporal discontinuities in the most inappropriate places: the minds of the first thinkers to present characteristically modern ideas. Because ideas develop out of and in response to other ideas, the location of the modern break in the thought of one philosopher or another can easily be refuted and the "origins" of modernity pushed further and further back in time.

15. H. Blumenberg, *The Legitimacy of the Modern Age,* 137–43. Blumenberg's conception of the "self-assertion" of reason is an especially helpful way of characterizing the new theoretical attitude because it captures the element of subjectivity or self-assertion that inspires this distinctively modern form of rationalism. Rationalism and subjectivity, many theorists (like Alain Touraine in *Critique of Modernity*) have argued, are the yin and yang of distinctly modern attitudes. Blumenberg's characterization of modern thought shows how they work together right from the beginning.

16. I examine this peculiar characterization of modernity as a project more fully and critically in Chapter 5. Let me merely note here that the description of modernity, or even the Enlightenment, as a project, does not emerge until rather late, not before the 1930s.

17. For a helpful contrast between modernity as a social condition and as a state of mind, see N. Rengger, *Political Theory, Modernity, and Postmodernity.*

18. For examples of recent work along these lines, see A. Giddens, *The Consequences of Modernity,* U. Beck, *Risk Society,* and P. Wagner, *A Sociology of Modernity.* Wagner's book, in effect, tries to provide the sociology behind the political conception of modernity. Alain Touraine's recent book, *Critique of Modernity,* explores the philosophical and sociological conceptions together.

19. K. Marx and F. Engels, *The Communist Manifesto*, 476.

20. See, for example, F. Feher, ed., *The French Revolution and the Birth of Modernity*.

21. C. Baudelaire, *The Painter of Modern Life and Other Essays*, 13.

22. I discuss the relationship between modernism and modernity more extensively in Chapter 3.

23. It is this feature of aesthetic modernism that makes it seem so plausible to treat postmodernism as the continuation of modernism rather than its reversal, as an illustration of the modernist spirit of innovation and tradition-smashing turning on its own modernist orthodoxies.

24. See M. Callinescu, *Five Faces of Modernity*, 41–46, for a nice discussion of the tension between "aesthetic" and "bourgeois modernity." There is, one should note, an alternative sociological conception of modernity, developed by Georg Simmel among others, that better corresponds to the aesthetic conception. See D. Frisby, *Fragments of Modernity*.

25. H. Jonas, "The Scientific and Technological Revolution," 51.

26. E. Gellner, *Postmodernism, Reason, and Religion*, 94. According to Gellner, for whom the concept of "industrial society" captures the distinctive features of distinctly modern ideas and practices, modern societies unavoidably rely upon "a pre-industrial idiom of legitimation."

27. Ibid.

28. See J. Habermas, "Modernity vs. Postmodernity," and *The Philosophical Discourse of Modernity*.

29. D. Lyon, *Postmodernity*, vii.

30. A. Giddens, *The Consequences of Modernity*, 139.

31. R. Musil, "Helpless Europe," in Musil, *Precision and Soul*, 122.

Two.   From the Moderns to Modernity

1. See M. Callinescu, *The Five Faces of Modernity*, 13–15; E. R. Curtius, *European Literature and the Latin Middle Ages*, 119.

2. See, for example, A. Touraine, *Critique of Modernity,* 62.

3. B. Yack, *The Longing for Total Revolution,* Chapter 3, "The Social Discontent of the Kantian Left."

4. Of course the classic social theorists are also interested in cultural and political diagnosis and the left Kantians are also interested in social explanation. (Marx, perhaps more than anyone else, fuses both interests.) I am merely focusing on the primary interest expressed in most of their work.

5. Hegel's story is unusual among left Kantians. He starts out, like the left Kantians, seeking to diagnose the ills of modernity by constructing comparisons with ancient Greek life. But as he grew older he began to believe that the very source of modernity's problems, the assertion of subjective freedom, eventually generates its own cures. As a result, he moved from the role of diagnostician to explicator of modernity as his career developed. See B. Yack, *The Longing for Total Revolution,* Chapter 5.

6. W. Welsch, *Unsere Postmoderne Moderne,* 67–68.

7. H. Blumenberg, *The Legitimacy of the Modern Age,* 473.

8. G.W. F. Hegel, *The Difference between the Systems of Fichte and Schelling,* 91. We need to "recompense nature for the mishandling suffered in Kant's and Fichte's systems, and set reason in harmony with nature, not by having it renounce itself or become an insipid imitator of nature, but by reason recasting itself into nature out of its own inner strength" (83).

9. F. Schiller, *Letters on the Aesthetic Education of Mankind,* Letter 6, 40–41.

10. F. Nietzsche, *The Uses and Disadvantages of History for Life,* in *Untimely Meditations,* 79.

11. I describe this group of philosophers and social critics as left Kantians because of the way in which they react to Kant's dichotomy between human freedom and natural necessity. They define their task as finding a way of realizing in the world the kind of moral autonomy that Kant portrayed as the distinctive quality that gives human beings their special dignity. A "right" Kantian reaction to this dichotomy would be to suggest that since moral autonomy is a quality of the noumenal will rather than the phe-

nomenal world, we must accept heteronomy, the subordination to traditional and personal authority, in our legal and political institutions. Kant's own position lies somewhere between these "left" and "right" wing interpretations of his legacy. See B. Yack, *The Longing for Total Revolution*, 98–118.

12. B. Willms, Introduction to J. G. Fichte, *Schriften zur Revolution*, 20. See my *The Longing for Total Revolution*, 108–18, for further examples of these parallels between the Kantian revolution in philosophy and the French Revolution in politics.

13. F. Schiller, *Aesthetic Education*, 24–25.

14. Ibid., 12–13, 8–9, 24–25.

15. Ibid., 12–13.

16. K. Marx, "On the Jewish Question," 44–46.

17. F. Schiller, *Aesthetic Education*, 204.

18. G.W. F. Hegel, *Theologische Jugendschriften*, 26–29. Translated in Hegel, *Three Essays*, 55–57.

19. F. Schiller, *Grace and Dignity*, 20:254–55, in Schiller, *Werke*.

20. Or as Hegel puts it, as "a matter of regional climate" this "dichotomy falls into the [modern] northwest" (*Difference Between the Systems*, 91–92).

21. F. Schiller, *On Naive and Sentimental Poetry*, 84.

22. The Rousseauian rhetoric invoked in this passage (see J. J. Rousseau, *Emile*, 40) reminds us that Rousseau anticipated many of these left Kantian insights and attitudes, as I argue in the first two chapters of *The Longing for Total Revolution*.

23. For the idea of a negative totality, see H. Marcuse, *Reason and Revolution*, 159, 313, and J. Grumley, *History and Totality: Radical Historicism from Hegel to Foucault*, 1, 207–8.

24. Similarly, in the English quarrel between ancients and moderns that preceded the French by a few decades, the major issue concerned the claims of the followers of Bacon that the new experimental sciences could surpass the achievements of the ancients. See R. Jones, *Ancients and Moderns: A Study of the Rise of the Scientific Movement in Seventeenth Century England*.

25. S. Huntington, "The Change to Change: Modernization, Development and Politics," 294.

26. For an account of both the partisans and the debunkers of the ancients on this issue, see B. Yack, *The Problems of a Political Animal*, 75–85.

27. L. Strauss, "Three Waves of Modernity," 83. See also T. McAlistair, *Revolt Against Modernity: Leo Strauss, Eric Voeglin, and the Search for a Postliberal Order.*

28. One possibility for such an ancient "project," suggested implicitly by Strauss and some of his followers, is the protection of philosophy from the hostility and persecution of religious authorities. But while this may be an important theme for some ancient philosophers, such as Plato and Lucretius, it clearly is not for others, such as Aristotle. The latter is so little concerned about the role of religious authorities that all he seems to have to say on the subject is that the priesthood is the appropriate office for citizens in his best regime to take up when they grow so old that they could use "a rest" from the active life they have led. See Aristotle, *Politics*, 1329a27.

29. I argue in *The Longing for Total Revolution* that it is ultimately a self-defeating challenge.

30. After the first wave of left Kantian speculation, ancient Greek models play less of a prominent role in this kind of social criticism, although it plays an important background role in the thinking of many later left Kantians, not least of all Marx. But every once in a while they return to prominence when you least expect it. For example, consider Henri Lefebvre's enthusiasm for the "myth of the new Greece" in his *Introduction to Modernity* (86–87, 226) and his hopes that the "proletariat" might try "to make it a reality." Ancient Greece, he suggests, still offers us "the only ideal and the only idea of man's possibilities"; it is the "yardstick against which we measure our own self-knowledge."

31. This paragraph draws on Yack, *The Longing for Total Revolution*, 125–32 ("The Three Waves of Left Kantian Speculation").

32. As formulated, respectively, by Henry Maine in *Ancient Law*, Ferdinand Tönnies in *Community and Society*, Emile

Durkheim in *The Division of Labor in Modern Society*. Weber also follows Tönnies by distinguishing between "associative [*gesell-schaftliche*]" and "communal [*gemeinschaftliche*] groups" in *Economy and Society*, 41–42.

33. P. Wagner, *A Sociology of Modernity*, ix. See also D. Sayer, *Capitalism and Modernity*, 11–12.

34. See C. Turner, *Modernity and Politics in the Work of Max Weber*, 61ff., 85.

35. M. Weber, *Economy and Society*, 41, 346.

36. C. Turner, *Modernity and Politics in the Work of Max Weber*, 32.

37. See N. Luhmann, *The Differentiation of Society*.

38. For critical accounts of the development of modernization theory, see J. Alexander, "Modern, Anti, Post, and Neo"; P. Wehling, *Die Moderne als Sozialmythos;* and S. Eisenstadt, Introduction, in Eisenstadt, ed., *Patterns of Modernity*.

39. See S. Huntington, "The Change to Change," 294.

40. See, for example, B. Latour, *We Never Have Been Modern*.

41. O. Lewis, "The Folk-Urban Ideal Types," 498.

42. See S. Huntington, "The Change to Change."

43. Modernization theory, however, has enjoyed a resurgence, inspired primarily by Niklas Luhmann's work in system theory, in German scholarship. For a thorough critique of the concept of modernity in contemporary German social theory, see P. Wehling, *Die Moderne als Sozialmythos*.

44. P. Wagner, *A Sociology of Modernity*, 24.

45. Ernest Gellner (*Nations and Nationalism*) and Benedict Anderson (*Imagined Communities*) are the leading modernists in recent work on nationalism. John Armstrong (*Nations before Nationalism*) and Walker Connor (*Ethnonationalism*) are among the leading primordialists. Anthony Smith's *Theories of Nationalism* and *The Ethnic Origins of Nations* tries to split the difference between the two camps. In Peter Wagner's *A Sociology of Modernity*, we find a typical modernist account of how the "idea of nation state was soon seized upon as the conceptually appropriate instrument for the imposition of modernity" (48).

46. Liah Greenfeld, in *Nationalism: Five Roads to Modernity*, challenges the modernist view but in a way that still maintains the sense that modernity must represent a coherent and integrated whole. Noting, correctly, that modern nationalism emerges in England and France, among other places, prior to the practices of industrial society that these scholars associate with modernity, she reverses their main argument and insists that nationalism is the source of modernity rather than modernity the source of nationalism. (See also L. Greenfeld, "Nationalism and Modernity.") For an assessment of the strengths and weaknesses of her argument, see B. Yack, "Reconciling Liberalism and Nationalism."

47. H. Arendt, *Eichmann in Jerusalem: A Report on the Banality of Evil.*

48. Z. Baumann, *Modernity and the Holocaust*, 93.

49. Ibid., 13, 17.

50. What makes modern technology and bureaucracy stand out from these other necessary conditions of the Holocaust is our initial identification of them with the forces of science and progress that we think of as the enemies of the Nazi regime. They catch our attention and encourage us to exaggerate their importance because their association with the Holocaust runs counter to our initial expectations. The same sense of surprise, I argue in Chapter 5, sustains the famous arguments about "the dialectic of enlightenment" made by Adorno and Horkheimer, arguments that, I shall argue, are no more plausible than Baumann's claims about the modernity of the Holocaust.

51. Hans Blumenberg makes a similar critique of secularization arguments in his book *The Legitimacy of the Modern Age* (30). These arguments, like the argument about the modernity of the Holocaust, assert the persistence of a particular way of thinking in a new development that appears, at first, to reject it. Secularization arguments insist that religious faith inspires, at least in a secularized form, much of the ideas and rhetoric of militantly atheistic philosophers and revolutionaries. Blumenberg points out that, in the end, these arguments rarely amount to more than asserting some feature of modern politics or philosophy is "un-

thinkable without" the religious attitudes that preceded it. "So much one would expect in advance of any deep inquiry. But what does it mean" with regard to the "concrete characteristics" of any particular case? Not very much, since there are so many nonreligious factors without which these features of modern politics or philosophy development are "unthinkable."

52. Z. Baumann, *Modernity and the Holocaust*, 93.

53. P. Wagner, *A Sociology of Modernity*, 69.

54. R. Musil, *The Man without Qualities*, 709.

55. H. Blumenberg, *Work on Myth*, 4–5. For an account of Blumenberg's argument on myth, see B. Yack, "Myth and Modernity: Hans Blumenberg's Reconstruction of Modern Theory."

56. That is why Herbert Schnadelbach ("Die Aktualität der 'Dialektik der Aufklärung,'" 241) describes the concept of modernity as a "social myth," as opposed to earlier myths about natural forces.

57. As Nietzsche suggests in *Untimely Meditations*, 64.

Three. Postmodernity: Figment of a Fetish

1. Many of postmodernism's problems could be avoided, from my point of view, if it changed its name. A great deal of confusion could be eliminated from the contemporary intellectual scene if we could come up with a name to characterize the skeptical, pluralist, and perspectival attitudes associated with postmodernism that did not identify them with the totalistic and self-contradictory beliefs about historical development that surround the idea of postmodernity.

2. See K. Kumar, *From Post-Industrial to Post-Modern Society*, 101.

3. See, for example, S. Seidman, Introduction, to Seidman, ed., *The Postmodern Turn*.

4. Among recent writings, see, for example, T. Pangle, *The Ennobling of Democracy: The Challenge of the Postmodern Era*, and R. Kirk, "Introduction" to Kirk, ed., *The Portable Conservative Reader*, xxxix.

5. D. Lyon, *Postmodernity*, vii.

6. A. Borgmann, *Crossing the Postmodern Divide*, 48.
7. J. F. Lyotard, *The Inhuman*, 34, 25.
8. Z. Baumann, *Intimations of Postmodernity*, vi–vii, 93.
9. J. F. Lyotard, *The Postmodern Condition*, 1ff; Z. Baumann, *Intimations of Postmodernity*, 187, 48–49.
10. For good accounts of the changing meanings of post-modernism, see H. Bertens, *The Idea of the Postmodern*, and W. Welsch, *Unsere Postmoderne Moderne*.
11. See Chapter 1 above for an outline of these different conceptions of modernity.
12. Mattei Callinescu (*Five Faces of Modernity*, 5–6) has a fine discussion of the conflict between the aesthetic modernity of the modernist movement and the "bourgeois modernity" of modern industrial society. See also K. Kumar, *From Post-Industrial to Post-Modern Society*, 85–87.
13. As the most insightful students of postmodern cultural movements have recognized. This insight leads Matei Callinescu to categorize postmodernism as one of *The Five Faces of Modernity* in his book of that title, and Wolfgang Welsch to title his study of postmodernism *Unsere Postmoderne Moderne (Our Post-modern Modernity)*.
14. F. Jameson, *Postmodernism, or the Cultural Logic of Late Capitalism*.
15. P. Osborne, *The Politics of Time*, vii.
16. One writer who does take these qualifications seriously is Ernst Behler, whose book is entitled *Irony and the Discourse of Modernity*.
17. A. Borgmann, *Crossing the Postmodern Divide*, 48.
18. J. F. Lyotard, *The Postmodern Condition*, xxiii–xxiv.
19. Ibid., 81–82.
20. On this point, see P. Wagner, *A Sociology of Modernity*, 75.
21. J. Gray, *Enlightenment's Wake*, 145; A. MacIntyre, *After Virtue*, 39. For a critique of the way in which MacIntyre constructs the "Enlightenment Project," see R. Wokler, "Projecting the Enlightenment."
22. Z. Baumann, *Intimations of Postmodernity*, 104.

23. J. Gray, *Enlightenment's Wake*, 145.

24. J. d'Alembert, *Preliminary Discourse to the Encyclopedia of Diderot*, 80.

25. Ibid. Similarly, Thomas Sprat's influential seventeeth-century account of the founding of the English Royal Society points to Bacon, rather than Descartes, as its guiding spirit. See R. Jones, *Ancients and Moderns*, 169, 223–24.

26. F. Bacon, Proemium to *The Great Instauration*, 424.

27. J. F. Lyotard, *The Postmodern Explained*, 83.

28. As do Lyotard, *The Postmodern Condition*, 1; M. A. Rose, *The Post-Modern and the Post-Industrial;* D. Lyon, *Postmodernity*, 37–38; and A. Borgmann, *Crossing the Postmodern Divide*, 60–61. For a clear and helpful discussion of this issue, see K. Kumar, *From Post-Industrial to Post-Modern Society*.

29. Z. Baumann, *Intimations of Postmodernity*, 95.

30. Ibid., 104.

31. See S. Seidman, *Contested Knowledge*, 315–16, for a similar complaint about the totalism of Baumann's portrait of modernity.

32. For this distinction between positive and negative totality, see J. Grumley, *History and Totality*, 207–8.

33. M. Jay, *Marxism and Totality*, 59.

34. See J. Grumley, *History and Totality*, 186–94.

35. V. Descombes, *Modern French Philosophy*, 181.

36. K. Marx, *The German Ideology*, 5:51.

37. F. Schiller, *Letters on Aesthetic Education*, Letter 5, 24–25.

38. I suspect, though, that they would have made a great deal of sense to Rousseau. See *The Longing for Total Revolution*, Chapters 1–2.

39. So I argue in the final chapters of *The Longing for Total Revolution*.

40. E. Gellner, *Postmodernism, Reason, and Religion*, 60–61.

41. Ibid., 61.

42. G. B. Smith, *Nietzsche, Heidegger, and the Transition to Postmodernity*, 135.

Four. What's Modern and What's Not in Liberal Democracy?

1. See Chapter 2 above.

2. C. Baudelaire, *The Painter of Modern Life*, 13. See also M. Callinescu, *Five Faces of Modernity*, 46–58.

3. K. Marx and F. Engels, *The Communist Manifesto*, 476.

4. M. Berman, *All That Is Solid Melts into Air: The Experience of Modernity*.

5. M. Berman, "Why Modernism Still Matters," 46.

6. I am not suggesting, however, that economic relations in advanced capitalist societies are thoroughly modern, that is, consistently dynamic, in their character. One could just as easily talk about "what's modern and what's not" in liberal capitalism as in liberal democracy, though I believe that more of contemporary capitalism than contemporary liberal democracy fits modernist models of ceaseless dynamism.

7. R. M. Unger, *Politics*. The three volumes in this work have the following separate titles: *Social Theory, False Necessity*, and *Plasticity into Power*. I shall refer to Unger's book in my notes by the titles of these three volumes.

8. "Trashing" is a word that the critical legal theorists use to describe their own activity. See M. Kelman, "Trashing," and, more generally, Kelman, *A Guide to Critical Legal Studies*.

9. R. M. Unger, *Social Theory*, 22.

10. R. M. Unger, *False Necessity*, 24, 572.

11. Ibid., 530.

12. Ibid., 24, 134.

13. Ibid., 575, 566.

14. For a full critique of Unger's vision of human emancipation, see my article "Toward a Free Marketplace of Social Institutions: Roberto Unger's Superliberal Theory of Human Emancipation."

15. R. M. Unger, *Social Theory*, 11.

16. See J. Habermas, "Modernity vs. Postmodernity." Habermas's original title, which was altered for this translation, was "Die Moderne—Ein Unvollendetes Projekt" ("Modernity—An Unfinished Project").

17. Ibid., 9

18. E. Gellner, *Postmodernism, Reason, and Religion*, 60–61.

19. It also, clearly, reflects the vision of reason and its appropriate uses laid out in Kant's three critiques: science as covered in *The Critique of Pure Reason;* morality as covered in *The Critique of Practical Reason;* and art as covered in *The Critique of Judgment.*

20. J. Habermas, "Citizenship and National Identity," in R. Beiner, *Theorizing Citizenship.* See also J. Habermas, *The New Conservatism,* 256–62.

21. For a critique of Habermas's argument about constitutional patriotism, see my article "The Myth of the Civic Nation."

22. I discuss the peculiar characterization of modernity as a "project" in the following chapter.

23. See C. Becker, *The Heavenly City of the Eighteenth-Century Philosophers,* and R. O. Rockwood, ed., *Carl Becker's Heavenly City Revisited.*

24. G. W. F. Hegel, *Vorlesungen über die Philosophie der Geschichte,* 926; partial translation, *Philosophy of History,* 447.

25. As W. Sewell notes, "one of the most important ideological products of the Revolution is the idea of revolution itself." W. Sewell, Jr., "Ideology and Social Revolution," 81. See also K. Baker, "Revolution," in Baker, Furet, and Lucas, *The French Revolution and the Birth of Modern Culture,* 1:41–62, and J. Baskiewicz, "La Révolution française aux yeux des révolutionnaires," for nice accounts of the revolutionaries' own reaction to this experience of revolution.

26. L. Hunt, *Politics, Culture, and Class,* 27.

27. F. Feher, Introduction, in Feher, ed., *The French Revolution and the Birth of Modernity,* 5.

28. F. Furet, *Interpreting the French Revolution,* 24, 204; L. Hunt, *Politics, Culture, and Class,* 2–3. See also Baker, Furet, and Lucas, *The French Revolution and the Birth of Modern Political Culture.*

29. F. Furet, *Interpreting the French Revolution,* 1–79.

30. Hamilton, Madison, and Jay, *The Federalist Papers,* #1 (Hamilton), p. 33; #49 (Madison), p. 314–15.

31. See B. Yack, *The Longing for Total Revolution,* 107–18.

32. Hamilton, Madison, and Jay, *The Federalist Papers*, #49, p. 314–15.

33. It is probably also appropriate to drop the image of the United States as the land of the future, where the brave new worlds promised by modern technology can first be experienced—as anyone who has been frustrated by the decaying infrastructure and public transportation of American cities will surely agree. Because the United States escaped the destruction rained on Germany and Japan, among other nations, during World War II, its cities appear, in many ways, much less modern than many of their European and Asian counterparts, despite their lack of monumental structures from the premodern world.

34. For a history of this image, see C. Van Woodward, *The Old World's New World*.

35. Quoted in ibid., 68.

36. J. Baudrillard, *America*, 29–30, 79, 90. On Baudrillard's *America* and on French intellectuals' views of the United States in general, see J.-P. Mathy, *Extrême Occident: French Intellectuals and America*.

37. Great Britain, America's predecessor as the paradigmatic modern nation, can, of course, boast of greater political continuity. But the continuity of the British political tradition today is accompanied by a sense of decline, and therefore alienation, that one does not find in the United States.

38. Though it is not, of course, seen in this way by most African Americans, who paid most of the price of the reintegration of the South into American political culture and the consequent reassertion of the continuity of American history. On the way in which even civil wars can, when recalled from a safe distance, become a source of national cohesion and even fraternity, see Benedict Anderson's interesting remarks (in *Imagined Communities*, 199–203) on "the reassurance of fratricide."

39. For good discussions of the meaning of the rule of law, see J. Raz, "The Rule of Law and Its Virtue," and J. Shklar, "Political Theory and the Rule of Law."

40. Aristotle, *Politics*, 1269a20.

41. J. Bentham, *Handbook of Political Fallacies*, 199.

42. In Dworkin's case the backward-looking element is the sense that our political and legal traditions make up a coherent whole that can guide us to "right answers" in hard legal cases, even if specific laws and precedents in themselves cannot do so. See R. Dworkin, *Taking Rights Seriously* and *A Matter of Principle*, 9–71.

43. See J. Elster, *Ulysses and the Sirens*, and S. Holmes, "Precommitment and the Paradox of Democracy."

44. See B. Yack, "Toward a Free Marketplace of Social Institutions," 1967–70.

45. E. Gellner, *Conditions of Liberty: Civil Society and Its Rivals*, 104, 103–6.

46. See E. Gellner, "The Social Roots of Egalitarianism."

47. See M. Kammen, *A Machine That Would Go of Itself.*

Five.   Disentangling Theory and Practice in the Modern World

1. M. de Montaigne, *Essays*, "Of Cannibals," 152.

2. M. Heidegger, "The Age of the World Picture," 115. Of course, Heidegger himself would resist this characterization of his view since he tends to think of metaphysics as the manifestation of a deeper experience of being rather than as a product of conscious theorizing. He would never say that theory led us astray, no matter how much emphasis he places on the Platonic break with pre-Socratic philosophizing in his accounts of the origins of modern technology. Still, in almost all of his accounts of the fate of the modern world, Heidegger is led back to the break between pre- and post-Socratics, with nary an effort to find some nontheoretical source of the change in the way being is manifested in human thought and action. The Greek philosophers may only have registered something deeper than their own philosophizing in their theoretical discourse, according to Heidegger. But it is *their* discourse, *their* theoretical innovations that offer the key to our fate in Heidegger's narrative about the origins of modernity. Theory rules in Heidegger's picture of the post-

Socratic world, even if only as a stand-in for an otherwise imperceptible call of being.

3. A. Bloom, *The Closing of the American Mind*, 293.

4. See, for example, J. F. Lyotard, *The Postmodern Explained*, 18, and J. Habermas, "Modernity vs. Postmodernity." Habermas's article (whose original title was "Modernity—An Unfinished Project) is, more than any other single source, responsible for popularizing this expression beyond those educated in German, and especially Heideggerian, philosophical traditions. Around the same time (1981), Alisdair MacIntyre's *After Virtue* popularized the expression the "Enlightenment project" in a similar fashion. See R. Wokler, "Projecting the Enlightenment."

5. H. Blumenberg, *The Legitimacy of the Modern Age*, 116, 467–68.

6. H. Marcuse, *One-Dimensional Man*, xvi, 154.

7. Ibid., xvi.

8. See, for example, R. Faulkner, *Francis Bacon and the Project of Progress;* T. Adorno and M. Horkheimer, *The Dialectic of Enlightenment*, 3–7; Michael Oakeshott, "Rationalism in Politics," 18–21.

9. F. Bacon, *The Great Instauration*, in Bacon, *Selected Works*, 425.

10. Quoted in H. Brown, *Scientific Organization in Seventeenth-Century France*, 103.

11. See R. Jones, *Ancients and Moderns*, 148–80. See Daniel Defoe's late seventeenth-century account of "the general projecting humour of the [English] nation" in *An Essay upon Projects*, ii, 24, passim.

12. Swift himself, it should be noted, was the author of "A Project for the Advancement of Religion."

13. "Let not the projector pretend the public good, when he intends but to rob the rich and to cheat the poor." Quoted in *Oxford English Dictionary*, 12:602.

14. L. Strauss, "The Three Waves of Modernity"; A. Bloom, *The Closing of the American Mind*, 293. For a detailed story of how such a philosophic project could shape socioeconomic reality, see H. Caton, *The Politics of Progress*.

15. See, for example, A. Schutz, "Choosing among Projects of Action." *Philosophy and Phenomenological Research* 12 (1951): 161–84.

16. J.-P. Sartre, *Being and Nothingness,* 460, 469, 501. In *Search for a Method* (13–14, 91–92), Sartre tries to go beyond the individualism of *Being and Nothingness* and talks about a "human project" rather than just the "fundamental project" of different individuals.

17. M. Heidegger, *Being and Time,* sections 31–32.

18. M. Heidegger, *What Is a Thing?* 93–97. Accordingly, Heidegger describes this realm as the "mathematical project."

19. M. Heidegger, *Nietzsche,* 4:28.

20. Ibid., 4:99.

21. M. Heidegger, "The Question Concerning Technology," 16.

22. I. Kant, *Critique of Practical Reason,* 166.

23. M. Heidegger, "Only a God Can Save Us," in R. Wolin, *The Heidegger Controversy,* 106.

24. Hegel, I suppose, is an exception here among speculative philosophers. Heine claims that, when he bubbled on about the eternity of the heavens, Hegel chided him for his childishness and dismissed the stars contemptuously as nothing but "the heavens' shining scabs." See H. Heine, *Geständnisse,* 3:365–66.

25. M. Heidegger, "Only a God Can Save Us," 105–6.

26. M. Heidegger, "The Age of the World Picture," 115.

27. The fact that what so excited these chemists about these molecules was their spherical shape—the most perfect geometric form in ancient Greek speculation—makes it an especially nice illustration of continuity with older contemplative attitudes toward nature.

28. H. Blumenberg, *The Legitimacy of the Modern Age,* 473.

29. E. Gellner, *Postmodernism, Reason, and Religion,* 59.

30. N. S. Love, *Marx, Nietzsche, and Modernity,* 195.

31. F. Fukuyama, *The End of History and the Last Man.*

32. See the critique of Adorno and Horkheimer's argument about the dialectic of enlightenment in J. Herf, *Reactionary Modernism,* ix.

33. "We must avoid the fallacy that in the last decades has frequently been used as a substitute for the *reductio ad absurdum:* the *reductio ad Hitlerum.* A view is not refuted by the fact that it happens to have been shared by Hitler" (L. Strauss, *Natural Right and History,* 42–43).

34. A. Hirschman, *The Rhetoric of Reaction,* 11–12.

35. A. Bloom, *The Closing of the American Mind,* 95–97.

36. See B. Wolfe, *Marxism: 100 Years in the Life of a Doctrine,* 322–23, for evidence that Marx, who usually was scrupulous about statistical evidence, had suppressed such information about rising wage rates.

37. Such as the arguments advanced by Ulrich Beck and Anthony Giddens that we are entering a period of more cautious or "reflexive modernization," a period in which modernity's skeptical rationalism is turned on itself and employed to rein in the excesses of distinctly modern ideas and practices. See U. Beck, *Risk Society* and U. Beck, A. Giddens, and S. Lash, *Reflexive Modernization.*

38. See B. Yack, *The Longing for Total Revolution,* 24–27.

39. R. Musil, "Helpless Europe," in Musil, *Precision and Soul,* 122.

40. M. de Montaigne, *Essays,* "Of Cannibals," 152.

41. A. MacIntyre, *After Virtue,* 61.

42. Ibid. Theory and practice so consistently embody each other for MacIntyre that he assumes the disagreements between leading philosophers, like Rawls and Nozick in contemporary America or Plato and Thucydides in ancient Athens, provide an accurate guide to the central social conflicts of a society. See *After Virtue,* 244–51, for his account of social disagreement in America, and *Whose Justice? Which Rationality?* 42, for his account of disagreement in ancient Athens.

43. M. Sandel, "The Procedural Republic and the Unencumbered Self," 81, 95.

44. It is, Sandel writes, "as if the unencumbered self has become true." He has to add this "as if" because according to his critique of liberal theory it cannot become true. See B. Yack, "Does Liberal Practice 'Live Down' to Liberal Theory?"

45. See B. Yack, "The Problem with Kantian Liberalism."

Ironically, both sides in this debate about Rawls and liberalism share the assumption that liberal theory and practice mirror each other as a coherent and integrated whole.

46. R. Musil, "Mind and Experience: Notes for Readers Who've Escaped the Decline of the West," in Musil, *Precision and Soul*, 137.

47. The problem with this form of skepticism is thus something more than the familiar difficulty that all skeptics have in justifying their claims to know that we cannot know certain things. Historicist critics of modernity, such as Heidegger and Adorno, claim to know something very important about the way things are, at least in the modern world, not just that we cannot know the things that many modern theorists claim to know.

Conclusion

1. See U. Beck, A. Giddens, and S. Lash, *Reflexive Modernization,* and U. Beck, *Risk Society: Towards a New Modernity.*

2. U. Beck et al., *Reflexive Modernization,* 2–3.

3. Ibid., 9.

4. The context in which Beck makes this claim concerns the judgment of environmental dangers. In this context, I would suggest, everyone has an interest in the consequences of economic practices, but expertise still carries a tremendous weight. It is just a different kind of expertise that comes into play, that of the biologist, the ecologist, or the doctor, rather than that of the plant manager or the microeconomist.

5. See the Introduction and Chapter 3 above.

Bibliography

Adorno, Theodor. *Minima Moralia: Reflections from a Damaged Life.* London: Verso, 1978.

Adorno, Theodor, and M. Horkheimer. *The Dialectic of Enlightenment.* New York: Continuum, 1982.

Alembert, Jean d'. *Preliminary Discourse to the Encyclopedia of Diderot.* Chicago: University of Chicago Press, 1995.

Alexander, Jeffrey. "Modern, Anti, Post, and Neo." In *Fin de Siècle Social Theory,* 6–64. London: Verso, 1995.

Anderson, Benedict. *Imagined Communities.* London: Verso, 1991.

Arendt, Hannah. *Eichmann in Jerusalem: A Report on the Banality of Evil.* New York: Viking, 1963.

Aristotle. *Politics.* Cambridge, Mass.: Loeb Classical Library, 1956.

Armstrong, J. A. *Nations before Nationalism.* Chapel Hill: University of North Carolina Press, 1982.

Bacon, Francis. *Selected Works.* New York: Modern Library, n.d.

Baker, Keith, F. Furet, and C. Lucas. *The French Revolution and the Birth of Modern Culture.* 3 vols. New York: Pergamon, 1987–89.

Baskiewicz, Bruno. "La Révolution française aux yeux des révolutionnaires." *Acta Poloniae Historica* 37 (1978): 71–93.

Baudelaire, Charles. *The Painter of Modern Life and Other Essays.* London: Phaidon, 1964.

Baudrillard, Jean. *America.* London: Verso, 1988.

Baumann, Zygmunt. *Intimations of Postmodernity.* London: Routledge, 1992.

———. *Modernity and the Holocaust.* Ithaca: Cornell University Press, 1989.

Beck, Ulrich. *Risk Society: Towards a New Modernity.* London: Sage, 1992.

Beck, Ulrich, Anthony Giddens, and Scott Lash. *Reflexive Modernization*. Cambridge: Polity Press, 1994.

Becker, Carl. *The Heavenly City of the Eighteenth-Century Philosophers*. New York: Yale University Press, 1948.

Behler, Ernst. *Irony and the Discourse of Modernity*. Seattle: University of Washington Press, 1990.

Bentham, Jeremy. *Handbook of Political Fallacies*. Baltimore: Johns Hopkins University Press, 1952.

Berman, Marshall. *All That Is Solid Melts into Air: The Experience of Modernity*. New York: Penguin, 1988.

———. "Why Modernism Still Matters." In S. Lash and J. Friedman. eds., *Modernity and Identity*, 33–58. Oxford: Blackwell, 1992.

Bertens, Hans. *The Idea of the Postmodern*. London: Routledge, 1995.

Bloom, Allan. *The Closing of the American Mind: How Higher Education Has Failed Democracy and Impoverished the Souls of Today's Students*. New York: Simon & Schuster, 1987.

Blumenberg, Hans. *The Legitimacy of the Modern Age*. Cambridge, Mass.: MIT Press, 1983.

———. *Work on Myth*. Cambridge, Mass.: MIT Press, 1985.

Borgmann, Albert. *Crossing the Postmodern Divide*. Chicago: University of Chicago Press, 1992.

Bouveresse, Jacques. *Rationalité et cynisme*. Paris: Editions de Minuit, 1984.

Brown, Harcourt. *Scientific Organization in Seventeenth-Century France*. New York: Russell and Russell, 1967.

Callinescu, Matei. *The Five Faces of Modernity*. Durham: Duke University Press, 1987.

Caton, Hiram. *The Politics of Progress*. Gainesville: University of Florida Press, 1988.

Connolly, William E. *Political Theory and Modernity*. Ithaca: Cornell University Press, 1993.

Connor, Walker. *Ethnonationalism*. Princeton: Princeton University Press, 1994.

Curtius, E. R. *European Literature and the Latin Middle Ages*. New York: Harper and Row, 1964.

Defoe, Daniel. *An Essay upon Projects.* Menston, England: The Scholar Press Limited, 1969. (Facsimile of 1697 edition.)

Descombes, Vincent. *Modern French Philosophy.* Cambridge: Cambridge University Press, 1988.

Durkheim, Emile. *The Division of Labor in Modern Society.* New York: The Free Press, 1964.

Dworkin, Ronald. *A Matter of Principle.* Cambridge, Mass.: Harvard University Press, 1985.

———. *Taking Rights Seriously.* Cambridge, Mass.: Harvard University Press, 1977.

Eisenstadt, S. N. Introduction. In Eisenstadt, ed., *Patterns of Modernity.* Volume 1: *The West,* 1–11. New York: New York University Press, 1987.

Elster, Jon. *Ulysses and the Sirens.* Cambridge: Cambridge University Press, 1979.

Faulkner, Robert. *Francis Bacon and the Project of Progress.* Lanham, Md.: Rowman & Littlefield, 1993.

Feher, Ferenc, ed., *The French Revolution and the Birth of Modernity.* Berkeley: University of California Press, 1990.

Feenberg, Andrew. *Alternative Modernity.* Berkeley: University of California Press, 1995.

Foucault, Michel. "What Is Enlightenment?" In *The Foucault Reader.* New York: Pantheon, 1990.

Frisby, David. *Fragments of Modernity: Theories of Modernity in the Works of Simmel, Kracauer and Benjamin.* Cambridge: Polity Press, 1985.

Fukuyama, Francis. *The End of History and the Last Man.* New York: The Free Press, 1992.

Furet, François. *Interpreting the French Revolution.* Cambridge: Cambridge University Press, 1981.

Gellner, Ernest. *Conditions of Liberty: Civil Society and Its Rivals.* London: Penguin, 1994.

———. *Legitimation of Belief.* Cambridge: Cambridge University Press, 1979.

———. *Nations and Nationalism.* Ithaca: Cornell University Press, 1983.

———. *Postmodernism, Reason, and Religion*. London: Routledge, 1992.

———. "The Social Roots of Egalitarianism." In Gellner, *Culture, Identity, and Politics*, 91–110. Cambridge: Cambridge University Press, 1987.

Giddens, Anthony. *The Consequences of Modernity*. Stanford: Stanford University Press, 1990.

Gray, John. *Enlightenment's Wake*. London: Routledge, 1995.

Greenfeld, Liah. *Nationalism: Five Roads to Modernity*. Cambridge, Mass.: Harvard University Press, 1992.

———. "Nationalism and Modernity." *Social Research* 63 (1996): 3–40.

Grumley, John. *History and Totality: Radical Historicism from Hegel to Foucault*. London: Routledge, 1989.

Gumbrecht, H.-U. "Modern, Modernität, Moderne." In O. Brunner, O. Conze, and R. Koselleck, eds., *Geschichtliche Grundbegriff*. 8 vols. 4:93–131. Stuttgart, 1978.

Habermas, Jürgen. "Citizenship and National Identity." In R. Beiner, *Theorizing Citizenship*. Albany: SUNY Press, 1995, 255–82.

———. "Modernity vs. Postmodernity." *New German Critique* 33 (1981): 3–14.

———. *The New Conservatism*. Cambridge, Mass.: MIT Press, 1989.

———. *The Philosophical Discourse of Modernity*. Cambridge, Mass.: MIT Press, 1987.

Hamilton, Alexander, James Madison, and John Jay. *The Federalist Papers*. New York: Mentor, 1981.

Hamilton, Alisdair. *The Appeal of Fascism*. New York: Macmillan, 1971.

Harvey, David. *The Condition of Postmodernity*. Oxford: Blackwell, 1989.

Hegel, G. W. F. *The Difference between the Systems of Fichte and Schelling*. Albany: SUNY Press, 1977.

———. *Philosophy of History*. New York: Dover, 1956.

———. *Theologische Jugendschriften*. Tübingen, 1908.

————. *Three Essays.* Notre Dame, Ind.: Notre Dame University Press, 1984.

————. *Vorlesungen über die Philosophie der Geschichte.* Hamburg, 1976.

Heidegger, Martin. "The Age of the World Picture" and "The Question Concerning Technology." In Heidegger, *The Question Concerning Technology and Other Essays.* New York: Harper, 1977.

————. *Being and Time.* New York: Harper, 1965.

————. *Nietzsche.* 4 vols. New York: Harper, 1979–87.

————. "Only a God Can Save Us." In R. Wolin, *The Heidegger Controversy,* 91–116. Cambridge, Mass.: MIT Press, 1993.

————. *What Is a Thing?* Chicago: Gateway, 1967.

Heine, Heinrich. *Geständnisse.* In Heine, *Sämlichte Werke.* 10 Bde., 3:323–97. Munich and Leipzig: Rössl, 1923.

Herf, Jeffrey. *Reactionary Modernism.* Cambridge: Cambridge University Press, 1984.

Hirschman, Albert. *The Rhetoric of Reaction.* Cambridge, Mass.: Harvard University Press, 1991.

Holmes, Stephen. "Precommitment and the Paradox of Democracy." In J. Elster and R. Slagstad, eds., *Constitutionalism and Democracy,* 195–240. Cambridge: Cambridge University Press, 1988.

Hunt, Lynn. *Politics, Culture, and Class in the French Revolution.* Berkeley: University of California Press, 1984.

Huntington, Samuel. "The Change to Change: Modernization, Development and Politics." *Comparative Politics* (1971):283–322.

Jameson, Fredric. *Postmodernism, or the Cultural Logic of Late Capitalism.* London, Verso, 1991.

Jauss, H. R. "Literärische Tradition und gegenwärtiges Bewusstsein der Modernität." In Jauss, *Literaturgeschichte als Provokation.* Frankfurt: Suhrkamp, 1970.

Jay, Martin. *Marxism and Totality.* Berkeley: University of California Press, 1984.

Jehlen, Myra. *American Incarnation: Nation, Individual, and Continent.* Cambridge, Mass.: Harvard University Press, 1986.

Jonas, Hans. "The Scientific and Technological Revolution." In H. Jonas, *Philosophical Essays*, 45–80. Chicago: University of Chicago Press, 1974.

Jones, Richard. *Ancients and Moderns: A Study of the Rise of the Scientific Movement in Seventeenth-Century England.* St. Louis: Washington University Studies, 1961.

Kammen, Michael. *A Machine That Would Go of Itself.* New York: Vintage, 1987.

Kant, Immanuel. *The Critique of Judgment.* New York: Hafner, 1968.

———. *The Critique of Practical Reason.* Indianapolis: Bobbs-Merrill, 1956.

———. *The Critique of Pure Reason.* New York: St. Martin's Press, 1965.

Kelman, Mark. *A Guide to Critical Legal Studies.* Cambridge, Mass.: Harvard University Press, 1987.

———. "Trashing." *Stanford Law Review* 36 (1984): 291–338.

Kirk, Russell, ed. *The Portable Conservative Reader.* New York: Penguin, 1982.

Kolb, David. *The Critique of Pure Modernity.* Chicago: University of Chicago Press, 1986.

Koselleck, Reinhart. "*Neuzeit*: Remarks on the Modern Conception of Movement." In Koselleck, *Futures Past*, 231–66. Cambridge, Mass.: MIT Press, 1985.

Kumar, Krishan. *From Post-Industrial to Post-Modern Society.* Oxford: Blackwell, 1995.

Latour, Bruno. *We Never Have Been Modern.* Cambridge, Mass.: Harvard University Press, 1994.

Lefebvre, Henri. *Introduction to Modernity.* London: Verso, 1995.

Le Goff, Jacques. *History and Memory.* New York: Columbia University Press, 1992.

Lewis, Oscar, "The Folk-Urban Ideal Types." In P. Hauser and L. Schnore, eds., *The Study of Urbanization*, 491–517. New York: John Wiley, 1965.

Love, Nancy S. *Marx, Nietzsche, and Modernity.* New York: Columbia University Press, 1986.

Luhmann, Niklas. *The Differentiation of Society.* New York: Columbia University Press, 1982.

Lyon, David. *Postmodernity.* Minneapolis: University of Minnesota Press, 1994.

Lyotard, Jean François. *The Inhuman.* Stanford: Stanford University Press, 1991.

————. *The Postmodern Condition.* Minneapolis: University of Minnesota Press, 1984.

————. *The Postmodern Explained.* Minneapolis: University of Minnesota Press, 1992.

MacIntyre, Alisdair. *After Virtue,* 2d edition. Notre Dame, Ind.: Notre Dame University Press, 1984.

————. *Whose Justice? Which Rationality?* Notre Dame, Ind.: Notre Dame University Press, 1988.

Maine, Henry. *Ancient Law.* Boston: Beacon Press, 1963.

Marcuse, Herbert. *One-Dimensional Man.* Boston: Beacon Press, 1964.

————. *Reason and Revolution.* Boston: Beacon Press, 1960.

Marx, Karl. *Capital.* New York: Modern Library, n.d.

————. *The German Ideology.* In Marx and Engels, *Collected Works,* 5:19–540. New York: International Publishers, 1975–.

————. *The Communist Manifesto.* In R. Tucker, ed., *The Marx-Engels Reader,* 469–500. New York: Norton, 1978.

————. "On the Jewish Question." In R. Tucker, ed., *The Marx-Engels Reader,* 26–53.

Mathy, Jean-Philippe. *Extrême-Occident: French Intellectuals and America.* Chicago: University of Chicago Press, 1993.

McAlistair, Ted V. *Revolt Against Modernity: Leo Strauss, Eric Voeglin, and the Search for a Postliberal Order.* Lawrence: University of Kansas Press, 1996.

Megill, Allen. *Prophets of Extremity.* Berkeley: University of California Press, 1985.

Merton, Robert. *On the Shoulders of Giants.* Chicago: University of Chicago Press, 1993.

Montaigne, Michel de. *Essays.* Trans. Donald Frame. Stanford: Stanford University Press, 1965.

Musil, Robert. *The Man Without Qualities*. New York: Knopf, 1995.

———. *Precision and Soul*. Chicago: University of Chicago Press, 1994.

Nietzsche, Friedrich. *Untimely Meditations*. Cambridge: Cambridge University Press, 1983.

Oakeshott, Michael. "Rationalism in Politics." In Oakeshott, *Rationalism in Politics and Other Essays*, 5–42. Indianapolis: Liberty Fund Press, 1993.

Osborne, Peter. *The Politics of Time*. London: Verso, 1995.

Pangle, Thomas. *The Ennobling of Democracy: The Challenge of the Postmodern Era*. Baltimore: Johns Hopkins University Press, 1992.

Pippin, Robert. *Modernism as a Philosophical Problem*. Oxford: Blackwell, 1991.

Raz, Joseph. "The Rule of Law and Its Virtue." In Raz, *The Authority of Law*, 210–29. Oxford: Clarendon Press, 1979.

Rengger, N. J. *Political Theory, Modernity, and Postmodernity*. Oxford: Blackwell, 1995.

Rockwood, R. O., ed., *Carl Becker's "Heavenly City" Revisited*. Ithaca: Cornell University Press, 1956.

Rorty, Richard. "Habermas and Lyotard on Postmodernity." In S. Lash and J. Friedman, eds., *Modernity and Identity*, 59–72. Oxford: Blackwell, 1992.

Rose, M. A. *The Post-Modern and the Post-Industrial*. Cambridge: Cambridge University Press, 1991.

Rousseau, Jean-Jacques. *Emile*, 40. New York: Basic Books, 1966.

Sandel, M. "The Procedural Republic and the Unencumbered Source." *Political Theory* 12 (1984): 81–96.

Sartre, Jean-Paul. *Being and Nothingness*. New York: Washington Square Press, 1966.

———. *Search for a Method*. New York: Vintage, 1968.

Sayer, Derek. *Capitalism and Modernity*. London: Routledge, 1991.

Schelling, Friedrich. "New Deduction of Natural Right." In Schelling, *On the Unconditional in Human Knowledge: Four Essays*. Lewisburg: Bucknell University Press, 1980.

Schiller, Friedrich. *Letters on the Aesthetic Education of Mankind.* Oxford: Oxford University Press, 1967.

———. *On Naive and Sentimental Poetry.* New York: Ungar, 1966.

———. *Werke,* ed. L. Blumenthal and B. von Wiese. Weimar, 1943–.

Schnädelbach, Herbert. "Die Aktualität der 'Dialektik der Aufklärung'" and "Gescheiterte Moderne?" in Schnädelbach, *Zur Rehabilitierung des Animal Rationale,* 231–50 and 431–46. Frankfurt: Suhrkamp, 1990.

Schutz, Alfred. "Choosing among Projects of Action." *Philosophy and Phenomenological Research* 12 (1951): 161–84.

Seidman, Steven. *Contested Knowledge.* Oxford: Blackwell, 1994.

———. "The End of Sociological Theory," 119–39. In Seidman, ed., *The Postmodern Turn.* Cambridge: Cambridge University Press, 1995.

Sewell, W., Jr. "Ideology and Social Revolution." *Journal of Modern History* 57 (1985): 57–85.

Shklar, Judith. "Political Theory and the Rule of Law." In *The Rule of Law: Ideal or Illusion,* 1–16. Ed. A. Hutchinson and P. Monahan. Toronto: Carswell, 1987.

Smith, Anthony. *The Ethnic Origins of Nations.* Oxford: Blackwell, 1986.

———. *Theories of Nationalism.* New York: Holmes & Meier, 1983.

Smith, Gregory Bruce. *Nietzsche, Heidegger, and the Transition to Postmodernity.* Chicago: University of Chicago Press, 1995.

Strauss, Leo. *Natural Right and History.* Chicago: University of Chicago Press, 1953.

———. "Three Waves of Modernity," In Strauss. *An Introduction to Political Philosophy: Ten Essays.* Detroit: Wayne State University Press, 1989.

Tocqueville, Alexis de. *Democracy in America.* Garden City: Anchor, 1969.

Tönnies, Ferdinand. *Community and Society.* New York: Harper, 1963.

Toulmin, Stephen. *Cosmopolis: The Hidden Agenda of Modernity.* Chicago: University of Chicago Press, 1990.

Touraine, Alain. *Critique of Modernity.* Oxford: Blackwell, 1995.

Turner, Charles. *Modernity and Politics in the Work of Max Weber.* London: Routledge, 1992.

Unger, Roberto. *Politics.* 3 vols. Cambridge: Cambridge University Press, 1988.

Vattimo, Gianni. *The End of Modernity.* Baltimore: Johns Hopkins University Press, 1991.

———. *The Transparent Society.* Baltimore: Johns Hopkins University Press, 1992.

Wagner, Peter. *A Sociology of Modernity.* London: Routledge, 1994.

Weber, Max. *Economy and Society.* Berkeley: University of California Press, 1978.

Wehling, Peter. *Die Moderne als Sozialmythos.* Frankfurt: Campus Verlag, 1992.

Welsch, Wolfgang. *Unsere Postmoderne Moderne.* Fourth Edition. Akademie Verlag, 1993.

Willms, Bernard. Introduction to J. G. Fichte, *Schriften zur Revolution.* Frankfurt: Suhrkamp, 1967.

Wokler, Robert. "Projecting the Enlightenment." In R. Horton and S. Mendus, eds., *After MacIntyre,* 108–26. Notre Dame, Ind.: University of Notre Dame Press, 1994.

Wolfe, Bertram. *Marxism: 100 Years in the Life of a Doctrine.* New York: Dial Press, 1965.

Wolin, Richard. *The Politics of Being.* New York: Columbia University Press, 1990.

Woodward, C. Van. *The Old World's New World.* Oxford: Oxford University Press, 1990.

Yack, Bernard. "Does Liberal Practice 'Live Down' to Liberal Theory?" in C. Reynolds, ed., *Community in America: The Challenges of "Habits of the Heart,"* 149–67. Berkeley: University of California Press, 1988.

———. *The Longing for Total Revolution: Philosophic Sources of Social Discontent from Rousseau to Marx and Nietzsche.* Berkeley: University of California Press, 1992.

————. "The Myth of the Civic Nation." *Critical Review* 10 (1996): 193–211.

————. "Myth and Modernity: Hans Blumenberg's Reconstruction of Modern Theory." *Political Theory* 15 (May 1987): 244–61.

————. "The Problem with Kantian Liberalism." In R. Beiner and W. J. Booth, eds., *Kant and Political Philosophy: The Contemporary Legacy*, 244–64. New Haven: Yale University Press, 1993.

————. *The Problems of a Political Animal: Community, Conflict and Justice in Aristotelian Political Thought*. Berkeley: University of California Press, 1993.

————. "Reconciling Liberalism and Nationalism." *Political Theory* 23 (February 1995): 166–82.

————. "Toward a Free Marketplace of Social Institutions: Roberto Unger's Superliberal Theory of Human Emancipation." *Harvard Law Review* 101 (June 1988): 1961–77.

Index